ETHAN ALLEN®

HOME INTERIORS

MERRILLVILLE
8000 Broadway
Merrillville, IN 46410
(219) 769-6301
(800) 476-3647

MISHAWAKA
5225 North Main
Mishawaka, IN 46545
(574) 247-2700
(800) 476-3659

ETHAN ALLEN® style 1

CREATE THE LOOK YOU LOVE

ETHAN ALLEN® style

CREATE THE LOOK YOU LOVE

PRODUCED BY ETHAN ALLEN
TEXT BY KATHERINE ANN SAMON

ETHAN ALLEN MARKETING CORPORATION

Library of Congress Cataloging-in-Publication Data:
Ethan Allen Style: Create the Look You Love / by Ethan Allen with Katherine Ann Samon.

   1. Ethan Allen Marketing Corporation. 2. Interior decoration—United States.
I. Title: Ethan Allen Style: Create the Look You Love.
II. Samon, Katherine Ann III. Ethan Allen Marketing Corporation.
Library of Congress Control Number: 2002112986
ISBN 0-9725579-0-3
10 9 8 7 6 5 4 3 2
First Edition

contents

introduction

Envision opening the door to your home and seeing something astonishing: Your rooms, completely redone, from furnishings to accessories, in a style you love—and looking wonderful. And imagine knowing something else—that it's real. With this book, that transformation is truly within reach, in a process that's as enjoyable as it is easy to accomplish.

achieve unique style

In these pages you'll easily learn how to achieve a look that's beautiful and unique. Style today, more than ever, is about introducing well-considered furnishings into a room, avoiding a "matched" look, and generating the energy that comes from original room designs. That completed look is brought together with an overview and an experienced eye.

Everything you need to reach that goal, from start to finish, is contained in these pages. Consider this book one of the most valuable resources in your design library, the comprehensive reference you'll fill with articles and notes that pertain to your style. It's the source you'll turn to again and again, because it has the added benefit of helping guide you away from potential mistakes and directly toward everything you need to achieve that terrific effect—effortlessly.

prepare the way

Bringing a room together can give you a wonderful sense of

satisfaction, but for some people, getting started means first exploring two important issues.

The first is wondering whether having a beautifully furnished home is important. You know the answer if you've ever visited a home where the exterior was terrific, but the interior was overlooked as unimportant. A feeling of incompleteness probably affected your experience, because a home environment has significant impact on moods. The more inspiring and encouraging the atmosphere for relaxing, or for feeling energetic, or for spontaneous entertaining, the more apt you are to do or feel that very thing. There is an environment—from the simplest to the grandest—that will support the lifestyle and soothe the soul of each of us.

Second, budgets are an important concern. Remember that rooms don't have to happen this week—they can be built over time, starting with the most important components and adding slowly with a plan. This is where working with one of our in-house design consultants can be important, to discuss budget and design a complete room plan.

find your style

You're looking for the style that makes you feel thrilled and satisfied. To find yours, start turning the pages. There are twenty specific styles in this book, ranging from American to European, country to modern, and including Asian, Tuscan, Shaker, and Arts and Crafts—and one of them is sure to resonate with you. Then, consider whether the look is a match for not only your heart but also your lifestyle: Are collections of artifacts and beige tones ideal for a family with children and bounding pets? Is a style built around vintage fabrics a considerate fit for a partner who prefers tailored styles?

Let the idea, "I can picture us living there easily and happily" be a guide. The more a style supports your lifestyle, the more you'll appreciate it and revel not only in the look, but also in your efforts to make it come true. Spend time with the chapters, entering these design landscapes with pleasure and enjoyment, knowing they're leading toward the goal of achieving a stylishly comfortable home.

replace mystery with mastery

Taking the mystery out of interior design starts when you realize that every look is achievable. When you find a style in this book that appeals to you, you'll see that we've broken it down for you.

For each style you'll find a description of the look and the lifestyle, and a clear analysis of key furnishings and components. You'll understand why certain furnishings are chosen. For instance, you'll see that a Shaker-style dining area is built around a trestle table for its graphic shape as well as for its rural period interest. You'll find information on styles of furniture, upholstery, fabrics,

and color, as well as inspiration for positioning furniture and accessories. In addition, we've included historical information to put the design elements in context and give you background to begin your knowledgeable relationship with this style.

find the full potential

Knowing the backbone of a look is one thing, but what separates a stunning room—whether it's strikingly simple or dramatically detailed—from a pleasant room is the full effect. Full effect is about all aspects that bring a look to fruition.

And that's what this book includes: We've asked our designers to produce rooms that reach their full potential and provide rich atmosphere for every style, using the perfect window treatments, area rugs, art, and additional accessories. Then, we've assembled all the information for you: text that guides you through the steps, and sumptuous photographs that show precisely how the rooms are rounded out.

And we've gone the distance, showing you how paint, wallpaper, and architectural details such as molding and paneling can further transform a space.

enjoy the experience

The most important thing: Enjoy the process. Designing interiors for your home will be one of your most wonderfully gratifying experiences. After all, you're creating a home that not only looks pleasing, but also adds tremendous ease, practicality, and joy to your lifestyle.

Knowing that you're never alone in the design process will add to the enjoyment. Our in-house design consultants will be with you every step of the way: helping you get started, guiding you through the design process, adding suggestions and inspiration, and making the experience easy and fun, from beginning to end.

Ask anyone who has decorated a home: You'll feel tremendous pride and satisfaction every time you enter one of your rooms, and those feelings only become stronger every day. And they should. Because not only did you take the time to find a style that reflects you, but you also experienced developing it yourself. And that's where the pleasure and rewards are—living in rooms that you envisioned and that make you and your family feel terrific every day.

create the look you love

And all it takes is to turn the page—and begin taking part in the pleasure of reviewing exquisite rooms, and in deciding which style resonates most completely with you. Then, partnered with this book and our design staff, you'll be able to savor the experience of something marvelous: learning how to create the rewarding and terrifically beautiful look you love.

american formal

american beauty

Picture yourself savoring the embrace of a sumptuous wing chair, relaxing on a luxurious, leather-upholstered sleigh bed, or pulling beautiful Chippendale-style armchairs up to a sparkling dinner table that's been formally set.

While American formal furniture naturally has its roots in Europe, particularly in England, today it has an entirely new sophistication that's purely American, and that comes from elegant mixes and creative styling.

On the following pages, American classics take part in looks as varied as an elegant blue-and-white presentation, an aristocratic country-house lifestyle, a gracious new way with formal entertaining, an appreciation for early-American purity, and a glamorous new eclectic look.

Comfort, elegance, originality, and a direct approach to living—it's the absolute best of classic America.

15

formal mix

It's very clear—this family has arrived. At a lifestyle where even the most casual dinners feel sit-down glamorous; where impressive family rooms encourage relaxed living; where elegant bedrooms make a welcoming invitation. This look is about the freshness of blue and white, a worldly approach to mixing formal furniture, and a knowing eye for fine details. And most of all, it's about your eclectic sense of style.

fresh refinement

The elegance of these rooms comes from an open, airy styling not usually expected in formal rooms—and the confidence to pull it off. It's seen in the exposed tabletop, sans cloth; freshly picked delphiniums rather than a formal arrangement; French water bottles, not cut-glass pitchers; white accessories on a demilune rather than a silver tea service; and simple matchstick shades.

The combination of formality and innate ease is what gives these rooms their sophistication and warmth.

The structure of the look comes from:

- a mix of formal eighteenth century–style furniture with influences from a variety of countries—England, France, and Sweden—to create greater interest;

- contrasting wood tones—such as the white rims of French Louis XVI-inspired chairs and the dark-hued English-style dining table;

- floral themes in fabrics and art, bringing the outdoors into the rooms;

- an emphasis on comfort, selecting substantive pieces, nothing precious.

But the heart of the look is unmistakably the blue and white color theme, inspired by the beauty of a Chinese ginger jar. Usually associated with casual environments, its unexpected formal success adds to the appeal: in the pastoral feeling of the dining room's toile de Jouy; in the subdued energy of striped rugs; and in the warmth of plaids and florals for upholstery, linens, and pillows.

serene sophistication

In every room, expanses of white—the walls, the living room sofa, the dining room's demilune table, and the bedroom's occasional table and bed linens—enlarge the feeling of the spaces and provide serene contrast to the distinct lines of other furnishings. Accessories are also based on white—china, ceramics, lamps, and side tables— there are practically no glinting metal tones.

While blue and white china is easily associated with this theme because of its graceful patterns, chinoiserie also has impact—in the form of the ginger jar, and in some of the fabric design. Chinoiserie was fashionable in England from 1740 until the end of the century, brought into the spotlight by imports from the Orient. Popular patterns included latticework and pagodas, which were featured on wallpapers and fabrics. Landscape designers also picked up on the motif, incorporating chinoiserie into gardens in the form of small structures, bridges, or lattice-back benches. Thomas Chippendale, one of the most prominent eighteenth century furniture makers, integrated chinoiserie into his designs in the form of fretwork and lattice patterns. The elegance, intimacy, and warmth of chinoiserie accounts for its continued popularity today.

flawless accents

Art is hung lower than usual—only a few inches above the tops of the side tables—in the bedroom and dining room, allowing the eye a more natural resting spot. In the family room, the art climbs higher to balance the scale of more massive furnishings. The same sense of balance is seen in the bed linens, with layers of pillows balancing the silhouette of the bed as well as the strong toile de Jouy pattern of the chair.

how to create
the look

The success of this style starts with a mix of formal furniture in the style of eighteenth century England, France, and Sweden rather than simply from one country, adding a sense of uniqueness to the combinations. White and dark wood tones create depth, while a color theme of blue and white adds a more casual contrast in florals, stripes, plaids, and chinoiserie accents. An emphasis on white adds an airy quality, as does a more informal approach to accessories.

casual beauty

A relaxed floral theme runs through every room, linking the spaces, in everything from art to pillows. That informality appears in the blue and white mattress ticking that gives new interest to classics such as an English-style club chair.

keys to successful style

1 The sofa has skirting and exaggeratedly formal scroll arms, as well as having comfortable roominess. 2 Formal Louis XVI-style arm chairs are softened in white with blue and white toile de Jouy. 3 A Swedish-style demilune table, in an airy white, is moved out of a foyer and into the dining room as a remarkable serving piece. 4 The English-inspired bed, with its formal carving and four-poster design, is softened with beautiful blue and white fabrics. 5 The Chinese ginger jar that inspired the look displays a classic scene; almost all of the other ceramic, accent pieces are solid white to create a serene background. 6 In white wood rather than cut-crystal or brass, the lamp provides informality. 7 A Swedish-style library coffee table has a practical, open design and a white glaze over a light wood tone for a softer look.

1

2

3

4

5

6

7

the palette

The striking toile de Jouy pattern illustrates the blue and and white theme.

The formal bed is relaxed with plaids, unfussy tie closures, and petite florals.

White adds openness; the formal damask pattern is made casual in cotton.

The ginger jar's floral and outdoor scenes influenced the palette and artwork.

townhouse style

Just off Park Avenue, the street is lined with grand town-

houses. Walk up the steps to a regal front door, and turn the

key. Inside is a style for someone who's at home—country

or city—with impressive, timeless English pieces that seem

to have been handed down through generations; with opu-

lent textures and refined finishes; and with a simplified

American approach that's wonderfully to the manor born.

form and color

Classical shapes give Townhouse rooms their richness—silhouettes such as pediment mirrors, urn accessories, Regency-style lamps, and serpentine chests. Pairing black with golden tones, and bringing in sheen and glimmer, increases the feeling of opulence.

The elegance of a country house in the grand English tradition isn't restricted to country or suburban living. There can easily be urban reproductions of the country lifestyle. Wherever it occurs, the atmosphere is always the same—privileged yet beautifully welcoming, sumptuous but understated and comfortable, with an uncluttered look that's typical of classic American styling.

Townhouse style is about:

- the aristocratic presentation of eighteenth century-style English and French formal furniture;

- classic furniture shapes such as wing chairs, English-style sofas, serpentine chests, panel beds, and pedestal tables;

- impressive wood furniture details—gadrooning (an edging that's a series of convex and concave carved shapes), burl veneers and rich grains, medallion carvings, japanning, leather or marble tops, gold tooling, commanding molding, luggage-inspired handles;

- fabrics with stateliness: paisley, houndstooth, plaids, crests, riding scenes, and tapestry motifs.

The palette is strictly upper crust, in gold and tan, black and brown, with accents of rust, maintaining an underplayed elegance. The country-house theme continues with riding scenes and animal statuary.

depth of field

An unusually strong depth contributes to the rarified atmosphere. One way it's achieved is through richness of materials: the swirl veneers and leather top of the coffee table, the wing chair's paisley fabric, the textured leather of the sofa. Greater depth also derives from unusual layering: the japanned screen behind the sofa and in front of dark paneling; lush combinations of pillows and throws; and for the overmantel, a framed riding scene over an antique tapestry inset.

Finishing touches complete the patrician impression. Lighting reinforces the influence of large pieces such as the Regency- and nineteenth century-style bureaus and living room screen. Bed linens should be generously layered and repeat the palette, incorporating menswear patterns. Bring in additional textures such as the rattan of the side chair and include a round image, perhaps a bull's eye mirror, for interest.

Japanning (as on the living room chest and screen) was a means for finishes: a wood surface was coated with varnishes for a hard, brilliant finish. The ancient technique arrived in Europe in the 1600s, brought by Dutch traders who carried furniture to China to be decorated, and who brought artisans west. The use of japanned items adds depth to the period feeling of this room.

floor to ceiling

With the abundant richness of the furniture, finishes, and accessories, draperies and carpets require particular attention. In this style, they provide beauty and great balance. Sumptuous fabrics—the living room's silk, the bedroom's velvet—and valances with box pleats or simpler forms add necessary height to the rooms. Floors are covered in rich carpets that replay the idea of the grand English country houses, adding opulence and practical warmth.

29

Grand tours were once a rite of passage for young English gentlemen. And as is often the case in great English country houses that have passed through families, many of the treasures they hold were acquired generations ago: After the Renaissance, a young British gentleman would complete his grand tour of Europe, during which he would accumulate reminders of his trips that would also furnish his home. Upon his return to England, packing crates would arrive holding items as varied as furniture, paintings, drawings, architectural renderings, classical busts, tapestries, maps, clocks, and carpets.

classical consideration

Find ways to give classical shapes new appeal. Consider different finishes: The chandelier contains fresh sophistication in nickel tones rather than brass. Resist matching: Instead of chairs that exactly repeat the Regency-style table, slipper chairs with a Regency-inspired curve at the back are preferred, becoming further sophisticated in houndstooth upholstery. Including a cabinet in a different furniture style—this one was inspired by Hepplewhite—shows a range of knowledge.

how to create
the look

Townhouse style re-creates the aristocratic design found in England's grand country houses. The centerpiece is dignified and timeless eighteenth century English- and French-style formal furniture. Choose wood pieces with impressive details such as gadrooning and burl veneers, and decorative elements such as japanning and leather tops. Add upholstered pieces in classic shapes such as wing chairs and English-style sofas. Select stately fabrics such as tapestry motifs and paisley.

material riches

A rich range of materials and textures finds harmony in unified neutral tones and classical shapes—as in the wing chair with ball and claw feet, the carved fireplace surround, the coffee table, the faux leather tripod table, and the Aubusson-inspired carpet.

keys to successful style

1 A classic English-style sofa is ideal, bringing understatement in its profile, and richness in its crocodile-textured leather. 2 Lighting should enhance the style message, as does this Regency design with its muted nickel tones. 3 Reinforce the theme with art depicting country scenes, including some with leisure pursuits such as the hunt. 4 Choose wood furniture with impressive detailing, such as the marble top of this French Empire-style piece. 5 Build in comfort with pillows and throws, choosing some that reinforce artwork themes. 6 Details such as tufting deliver a refined message. 7 Incorporate rattan and caning into rooms to provide a fuller range of texture.

1

2

3

4

5

6

7

Draperies and wallpaper in rich golds are a stunning backdrop for black furnishings.

Textures play up an understated palette of gold, tan, brown, and black.

Houndstooth, a menswear fabric, underscores the gentlemanly approach.

Sumptuous burl veneers add an esteemed, through-the-generations quality.

gracious living

Letting beautiful fabrics shine adds the sparkle to this fresh

new look. It speaks to the heart of the person who finds

great pleasure in superb colors, patterns, and finishes for

fabrics; who marvels at how the rooms are transformed—

as if by an exquisitely talented dressmaker equipped with

trade secrets and exquisite materials—making them the

very best of well dressed.

dressmaker details

Two ways to see a dressmaker's mind at work: Simple curtains are transformed visually by pulling them open and tucking them behind higher-than-usual stays; slipcovers are re-imagined as a Martha Washington chair is dressed In a demure white damask slipcover that's been fashionably slit at the sides and fastened with discreet ties.

When decorating any room, an overall theme should be selected: here, it's about allowing splendid fabrics to create a looser, lighter effect with classic furniture. The way to this style:

- Colors must be decided—here, coral, rose, and cream for an airy elegance.

- Select at least two differently patterned or textured fabrics for an interesting mix—the smooth stripe and plush, solid-color velvet.

- A focal fabric is singled out—a muted floral, instead of a bright pattern or heavy brocade.

Once the pieces are in place, a focus on details is where the couture component can bring it all to its highest level: the intricate ruching at just the top curve of each sofa arm and a long bullion fringe that's as Victorian as it is boldly attention-getting. Tufting, piping, and flouncing—all three elements are brought to the ottoman. In contrast, the self-piping on the Louis XVI-style armchair is a precisely tailored accent.

perfect placement

The new approach for formal living: unmatched pieces and a more open floor plan that's ideal for entertaining. Rather than two sets of side tables and lamps, an asymmetric selection and positioning (the floor lamp is slightly behind the sofa) updates the formal look. An ottoman's softer, slimmer shape replaces a large coffee table. Floor-length draperies are belted low for the longest, most graceful line.

Details are the keys to the gracious feeling in this home. It's not about a large gathering of accessories, it's about the perfect finishing touches. In the bedroom, they add up to a feeling of eighteenth-century richness. Wallpaper —essential to this era—is in an opulent but subdued floral damask, the perfect backdrop for a dramatic bed. Appropriately, art is in the form of an intricate tapestry.

Muted colors mean a variety of elaborate materials and textures can come together in luxurious unity that even one bright note would interrupt. Illustrating the point: lamps, one with classic festooning and the other in an archetypal urn shape, are both richly finished and shaped, yet neither one tips the balance. Lavish textures finish the room, from the ornate smocking on the draperies to layer upon layer of elegant bedcoverings decked in the finery of silk trim, rosebud embroidery, braiding, quilting, and ribbons.

the age of indulgence

Grandeur—that's the inspiration behind the opulence of these rooms. To capture it in the bedroom, use sleigh- or poster-bed shapes. In general, instill importance with carved woods, tufted upholstery, swirl veneers, fluted legs, ornate hardware, and detailing such as the table's rich veneered ribbon patterning and ebony inlays.

The walls throughout this home are sparingly adorned with paintings, giving the rooms a more open feeling. In fact, in the Early Georgian periods, paintings were scarce, and so walls provided decoration with paneling, chair rails, and moldings. Starting in the 1740s with Britain's first wallpaper factory, paneling was omitted above the chair rail, and walls were decorated with silk or flock wallpaper, damask, or velvet. In the late Georgian period, colors such as corals, pinks, and yellows became popular, with wallpaper usurping fabric treatments. Here, the gently textured and toned wallpaper acts as a light background. Elegant Aubusson-inspired carpets in every room add strength to coral tones, enhance the mix of textures, and add a continental feeling.

luxurious layering

Groupings in specific textures, tones, and shapes can beautifully enrich a mood. Atop a Chippendale-style dressing chest, leather-bound books add period richness and become practical resting places for jewelry. A chaise is pulled into the room and angled for convenient resting, made further comfortable with an Aubusson-style pillow. On the bed, pillows with dressmaker details are piled high for complete luxury.

how to create
the look

A luxurious appreciation for fabrics and details gives these room lightened sophistication. Bring in dress-maker touches such as ruching and smocking, and thick fringe or ribbon trim to add a sumptuous finish. Look for new approaches to slipcovers and draperies that provide couture interest. Loosen up floor plans with asymmetric furniture arrangement. Turn to layers of details in harmonious colors to create depth and richness. Add opulence with furnishings that have fluting, swirl veneers, or inlays.

a view toward finery

Adding elegance to the room is a layered window treatment of sheer Roman shades and full-length draperies with elaborate smocking at the top. A tub chair shows the tufting and piping that help define this look.

keys to successful style

1 Sofas with touches such as moss fringe and generous bullion fringe announce intimate attention to details.   2 Recalling the beauty of the Georgian period are the urn shape and classic proportions of a Regency style lamp.   3 A more unique choice than traditional wall décor, a tap-estry adds a period effect.   4 Classic Louis XVI-style armchairs make a rarified contrast to heavier upholstered pieces, with an ease of mobility for entertaining.   5 A low-scale ottoman adds upholstered softness to a room and serves as a coffee table or extra seating.   6 A side table with classic Regency styling—clean-lined carving, and tapered, reeded legs—is a perfect choice for this look.

1

2

3

4

5

6

Elegant coral, cream, rose, and taupe add a lightened opulence to fabrics.

Luxurious detailing distinguishes draperies, upholstery, and pillows.

Pastel-tone Aubusson-style carpets send a rarified, timeless message.

Slipcovers contain dressmaker details such as open sides and tie closures.

period house

Afternoons in the parlor amid gleaming silver and rich dark woods, the lulling tick of a grandfather clock—it's a distinguished American home in the late eighteenth or early nineteenth century—following in England's fashion footsteps, but already finding a more open character. The beauty of Colonial American style shown here speaks to an appreciation of authentic shapes, textures, and colors—tying America's history with its most renowned classic style.

history notes

Martha Washington armchairs, Grandfather clocks, wing chairs, and brass sconces are part of the style, along with dark paneling and ornate rugs to epitomize dignity. Rooms are unfinished without candlesticks, brass or silver—here, the curved one is Georgian-style, the taller one Adam-style.

No two pieces of furniture establish Colonial American style as well as a camelback sofa and wing chair. At the height of their popularity, both pieces were found in the most refined rooms. The two reigning styles were Queen Anne and Georgian, with its top furniture makers Chippendale, Adam, and Sheraton. Although upholstered sofas—created for greater comfort than settees—were rare in the mid-1700s, this camelback shows the Chippendale influence in its ball-and-claw feet, while the rest of the room is of Queen Anne and American Federal styling.

To build the rooms:

- Look to reds and rusts for distinction, as well as to classic creams.

- In order to keep this look contemporized and fresh, substitute simple, light-filtering Roman shades for traditional swags and jabots.

- Use patterned carpets in as many rooms as possible to make an elegant base.

- Because a sense of culture was important to this era, botanical prints and full bookcases have a strong presence.

- Include tea accessories: The enjoyment of the drink created a small industry devoted to tea services and their attendants, such as the Adam-style tea caddy sitting regally on the table.

evolution of a style

Originally called the "confessional," the wing chair design originated in France, possibly earning its name because in profile its wide side pieces shield the face. The chair was further developed in England, and in the early 1700s found its way to America.

In England, it was a time of inventiveness for the home and the new leisure class—all of which found its way to American shores. Furniture was designed to be interchangeable: The same drop-leaf tables could be pulled into use for dining or card playing; likewise, chairs were meant to be shifted from the dining area to the parlor. Drawing rooms on the first floor were used for privacy as well as for receiving guests, and were the setting for the most fashionable part of the day—tea-time, which occurred several times daily.

Bedrooms were equipped for the art of letter writing, with a secretary often placed there for privacy. Secretaries began as two pieces, with a fall-front desk box sitting on a steadying table or chest. When they became one piece, drawers were added. Four-poster beds were frequently carved with rice or, as in this Federal style, wheat motifs.

treasury of textiles

Sleeping quarters expressed the same refinement as public rooms, particularly with drapery treatments—such as this contemporized tailored heading—and carpets. For the well-to-do in the late Georgian era, authoritative carpets by such esteemed designers as the Adam brothers, for instance, would mirror the intricate plasterwork that adorned their ceilings.

49

how to create
the look

Traditional style that imparts a sense of history is the heart of this home. Look to Queen Anne and Georgian-style pieces, and classic choices such as a camelback sofa and wing chairs, as well as furniture with the formal dressiness of mahogany-toned wood. Add pieces such as drop-leaf tables that have more than one function. Depend on reds and rusts to lend rich, aristocratic coloring to upholstery and carpets.

purity of form

In the foyer, setting the tone for traditional styling is a classic George I-style sideboard with cabriole legs and shell carving. The gold finish on the mahogany-finish mirror reflects the light gilding of the era.

keys to successful style

1 Look for period-appropriate artwork such as botanical prints. These are framed in deep oak burl veneer tones. **2** The styling of a French bouillotte lamp, with electrified candlelight, illuminates the period look. **3** Turn to the architectural style of chairs such as a Martha Washington to define the era. **4** Include candlesticks—once a necessity—to add atmosphere. **5** Drop-leaf tables such as this one demonstrate the leisure importance of the era and remain inherently practical. **6** The centerpiece of the look should be a sofa with historical stature and details, such as the Chippendale-inspired camelback sofa with stately ball-and-claw feet.

1

2

3

4

5

6

Choose fabrics such as damask to add texture and understated patterning.

Rich reds bring nobility to classics and elaborately woven textiles.

Beige window treatments, in simple linen, balance bold colors and shapes.

An elegant platform, carpets draw out the red and cream tones in the rooms.

51

american eclectic

Completely chic—that's the appeal of these elegant rooms.

If you gravitate to a range of periods and enjoy the unusual

alchemy that comes from bringing them together, this style

might be for you. The sum total tells about a person who

has an attractive range of interests, and who is drawn to a

more glamorous lifestyle—one that's as timeless as it is

of-the-moment.

spare formality

Past and present come together with clean, uncomplicated beauty: Chippendale-style chairs, with their carved-ribbon backs, pull up to a nineteenth-century English-inspired table—while opalescent faux leather brings glimmer to an updated club chair. Peaceful walls and simple blinds allow the mix to excel.

What makes this eclectic style so remarkable is the sharp contrast between traditional and modern furnishings. Although this effect feels spontaneous, it's anything but: It requires cohesion to succeed. Success depends on scale, proportion, and color—the fundamental statutes of style—creating a unified look.

Start with a well-defined color scheme for two strategies: Use the same fabric color to combine pieces of different eras such as the off-white sofas in the living room and the Chippendale-style chairs for the dining room. Choose solid color fabrics to enhance the lines of elaborate pieces without taking over the room.

The next steps:

- Introduce furnishings that balance each other, such as an intricate piece from one era and a simple one from another.

- Have a small but strong array of textures to give a room depth; for instance, the velvet Georgian-style wing chair is enlivened by one satiny orange pillow.

- Introduce an airiness with the glass of the lamp and the Deco-style table.

- Find intimacy through balance: The contemporized wing-back sofa has the breadth to hold its own with the stately upright traditional wing chair; Regency-style benches are positioned away from the coffee table for an open effect, yet are still within reach.

clean-lined living

A certain quality in a room can make furniture stand out, and that quality is derived from an emphasis on space and light. To achieve it, reduce the amount of furnishings and accessories in a space; focus on a neutral palette; keep windows bare, or use the simplest treatments; and utilize the space-enlarging quality of white for walls and rugs.

The way the furnishings are placed has a modern perspective: They're arranged more like gallery pieces, to allow concentration on their form and color, and they're meant to be viewed from any vantage point. In that light, the grand scale of the Empire-style sleigh bed feels at ease in a room with regular dimensions; pulled away from walls and angled—as is the contemporary club chair—it creates flow completely around it, and the illusion of additional space.

Focus on textures to enhance the mix: the bed's leather upholstery; the carved beading and fluting on the cabinet; quilting and menswear shirting fabrics on the bed; the easy pleating and slight puddling of the draperies combined with wooden blinds.

art appreciation

Just as furniture is given the same consideration as art, so are details. Choosing sculpture and drawings with neoclassical themes is a sophisticated, highly effective way to unite traditional and contemporary interiors. In a corner of the room, more artful accents: a marquetry table, and pillows in menswear vest fabrics.

how to create
the look

Mixing formal furniture in a range of styles creates unusual glamour—and requires attention to balance and scale. Use color to unite the styles. To make sure the rooms maintain their openness, turn to white to add a light, gallery quality to the spaces. Bring in an up-to-date component such as the opalescent faux leather. Neoclassical accessories bridge the eras.

eclectic elegance

Unexpected: The beauty of a modern club chair paired with a Regency style bench—one with the glint of opalescent fabric, the other with period-appropriate gilding. Simple walls and bare floors complete the modern interpretation of elegance.

keys to successful style

1 A Deco-style table updated with glass introduces period and modern themes.   2 Choose one large piece of art to make a dramatic statement.   3 A contemporized wing-back sofa is a modern take on a classic form.   4 A series of contemporary prints, hung in a row, becomes a single design element.   5 Contemporary accents show the impact of orange and the interplay of glass and metal.   6 Transcending time, a Chippendale-style chair makes a formal statement.   7 A sleigh bed's rich leather and carved wood are meant to be on full view.

1

2

EMMY MAGLiANI

3

4

5

6

7

Opalescent fabric gives a club chair its lightness and fashion sense.

A soft area rug incorporates neutral tones and texture from the ground up.

Popular in modern environments, orange accents add interest.

A quilted, patterned duvet cover is a tailored translation of damask brocades.

59

european
classics

the golden age

Imagine eighteenth century England: Acres of landscaped gardens, often with perfectly placed man-made ponds. Cabinet makers creating furniture of such design and quality that they sparked new styles. Craftsmen painstakingly inserting wafer-thin, contrasting pieces of wood into a chest's veneer to create designs—the art of marquetry.

That century elevated everyday life to an art form for wealthy Europeans. And with a rise in affluence, their homes approached a level of grandeur and detail formerly attainable only in palaces. On the following pages, Tuscan, Swedish, Caribbean, and British styles beautifully demonstrate the era's passion for decorative arts.

It was a time of unprecedented sophistication, quality, and romance that continues to set the pace for the way we want to live today—beautifully.

island
influences

The romance of the Caribbean can be transported anywhere—but it speaks specifically to someone who takes pleasure in natural textures such as woven grasses and rattan; enjoys lush wall colors such as coral and pineapple; and values beautifully sculpted furnishings. It's a captivating, loosened-up take on British and French classics—in a wonderfully original island style.

tropical mood

In the foyer, set the tone immediately with one strong piece—a French Regency-style console that has intricate Martinique-style carving. The gilded Louis XV inspired mirror has natural surroundings: flanked with banana-leaf wall sconces, supporting a palm print, reflecting tall fresh flowers. Shells and the woven rice container add to the mood.

The aim of this style: to feel the breezes, to imagine palm trees outside, to be transported to the late eighteenth century and, at the same time, feel very much today.

Island style is all about:

- rich mahogany tones—the European and island preference;

- furniture that has flamboyant island carving while presenting a lighter mood;

- natural-tone rugs instead of Aubusson or Persian;

- a mixing-in of rattan and woven furniture;

- an emphasis on plants;

- and whimsical touches such as banana-leaf sconces.

With sapphire skies and turquoise waters comes appreciation for climate: As heavy, cold-weather European attire gave way to tropical weight, so did the design, going simpler. Walls are the antithesis of French eighteenth century ornamentation—in classic island style, they're soothingly simple. Fabric patterns are less fussy. Colors for fabrics and walls are either a cooling white or refreshingly vibrant tropical colors.

learning new ways

The English-style barrister's bookcase is at home in new territory. Walls take their interest from simple planking infused with the appeal of coral-tone paint. Relaxed curtains pick up the color in an island-inspired fern pattern. A rattan lounge chair reinforces a relaxed Caribbean approach, while the lamp incorporates French styling with a casual leaf pattern. A woven rug is a tailored yet natural finish.

Island furniture evolved into its own distinct style. In the late eighteenth and early nineteenth centuries, England, France, Spain, Holland, and Denmark vied for control of the Caribbean islands. Legions of governors, officers, staffs, merchants, planters, and families arrived. High standards of living were reproduced by bringing over furnishings and importing from Europe and North America, but the islands' humidity and termites ravaged the pieces. Once local artisans were employed to reproduce the styles with native hardwoods, over time their work reflected their own rich motifs, such as the twisted rope seen on tables, chairs, and bedposts; and highly stylized pineapples and palm fronds. Consequently, each set of islands developed a distinct style that merged local tradition with the European style.

uninhibited style

To bring an exotic note to the dining room, a Regency-style table is chosen that has Jamaican rope-style legs. Under the French Regency-style lamp, a British-style curio cabinet shows a loosening of its Victorian heritage, as does the simplified tea cart. Design note: Inside the negative space on the side of each George III-style chair back is a clear outline of a bird in profile—a signature of this English-style chair.

69

For this style to succeed it relies as much on creating mood as it does on individual furnishings.

French doors are painted in a contrasting color to put the focus on the outdoors, with shutters to regulate light and suggest a tropical climate. With walls and doors painted in pineapple or coral tones to pick up the light, floors must have dark stain to provide elegant contrast. Art is minimal except for maps that have a far-flung feeling, and accessories such as the lamp, palm tree, and woven accessories to provide a new landscape.

trade route

The sleigh bed shows evolution to a simpler profile, with the omission of a footboard. Island reeding comes across on the headboard, on the Sheraton-style table with its faux bamboo bands, and on the mirror. Also chosen for its blend: a Regency-style lamp with a stylized palm tree motif. The bureau mixes French Empire and British campaign styles. Establishing British roots: an architectural brass lamp.

how to create
the look

This style is about a breezier, loosened approach to European classics, with heavily sculpted pieces pointing up the influence of a more whimsical island approach. Emphasize color, turning to vibrant, light-hearted tones. Introduce shutters to filter light in an island manner. Paired with rattan, classic English club styling effortlessly adds to the mood. Keep rugs simple in natural tones, and bring in nature with plants and plant motifs.

a corner of the Caribbean

Beautiful coral color envelops a room with Caribbean warmth. Accents are about simplicity in patterns—palm draperies, prints, and lamp—and in accessories—rattan, straw and wicker. Design note: The stylized pineapple was a favorite motif of West Indies craftsmen.

keys to successful style

1 Classic English club styling positions this sofa, but in island-weight white cotton rather than in a heavy wool or leather.   2 Stylized palm trees give these Regency-style lamps a more relaxed quality.   3 A French Regency-style table reflects the bold sculpting and flourishes of Martinique-style carving.   4 A palm plant overlaying an antique map sets the tone for exotic travel; sea grass matting adds island texture. 5 Woven boxes and accessories contribute hand-made artistry and the rich texture of natural materials.   6 As a contrast to mahogany-tone wood, a rattan and wicker-weave chair and ottoman with white cushions add a relaxed, more carefree quality.   7 A large-leaf palm tree beautifully re-creates the drama of the outdoors.

1

2

3

4

5

6

7

Paint establishes the locale with uninhibited color such as lemon or pineapple.

A coral color enriches the island theme and adds interest to palm patterns.

Bedcoverings show how classic toile patterns evolved into more lyrical styling.

With bold carving, island craftsmen transformed classic European pieces.

tuscany story

Out the window, the sun beats down on tall stands of cypress trees lining the drive to a villa. Olive groves and orange trees dot the surrounding terrain. Inside, fresh thyme lingers in the air, and a tenor's spirit-soaring aria fills the rooms. Tuscan style is about responding deeply to resplendent colors, masterful furniture, and opulent fabrics: A beautifully informal lifestyle, it celebrates the centuries —as well as the splendors of everyday life.

art history

Marquetry, most associated with the Renaissance and the court at Versailles, is often traced to royalty and wealth because of the fine craftsmanship required for its exacting application of decorative inlays and contrasting veneers. Here, sunburst marquetry turns a richly fluted and molded sideboard into a work of art.

Opulent and luxurious, Tuscan style is also emotionally rich in a way that's tied to the terrain and its place in history. That expressiveness comes from:

- a reference to ancient Roman design that's seen in the classical sense of balance and unity, and in motifs such as pediments, urns, and columns;

- formal eighteenth and nineteenth century Italian, French, and English furniture in full-tone woods that have rich finishes and hand-painted designs;

- boldly scaled wood furnishings—such as oval drum-shaped tables, bombé chests—with strong, classic detailing;

- an expansiveness that's reflected in plentiful objets d'art on mantels and tables—the very opposite of spartan.

Color is unmistakable in earth tones of olive green, terra cotta, ochre (brown-yellow), and umber (dark brown), along with creamy ivory, ever-present golden sun tones, and striking ruby accents. Upholstered pieces are ardently designed for comfort. Wrought iron (for chandeliers, tables), collections of bronzes and ornate altar candlesticks, and dynamically colored and textured draperies, fabrics, and carpets complete the sumptuous mood. Lampshades should cast an intimate, amber light over it all.

a sense of fulfillment

Fullness extends to the slightly rustic, Old World authenticity that architectural components should have: Add interest to walls with stucco or troweled textures. Use stone for mantels and floors— suggesting the ancient stone walls surrounding farmhouses and villas. Ceiling beams should be left unpainted.

The effect of Tuscan style rooms is often Renaissance in feeling: in the layering of velvets and silks; stripes, damask, and embroidery effects; trim in braiding and cartouche designs; an emphasis on ruby, moss green, cream, and gold.

The fifteenth and sixteenth centuries, during the Renaissance, comprised one of the greatest ages of intellectual and artistic enlightenment the world has known. Concentration was on ancient Roman studies; Latin and Greek classics, art, archeology, history, and architecture; investigating medicine, mathematics, and physics; and the study and execution of art and literature—and a reverence for both. Italy was one of the greatest centers, evidenced by the contributions of Leonardo da Vinci and Michelangelo. The symmetry, balance, and unity of a host of disciplines all came together, with their influences continuing to reach the highest levels of intellectual and artistic expression.

design disciplines

Classical values were an important part of eighteenth century design, as seen in urn shapes decorated with acanthus leaves and festooning; in the purity of a traditional, round, gold-leaf portrait frame; and in the symmetry and balance of the molding design on large furniture.

how to create
the look

Tuscan style centers on masterful furniture that has large, bold shapes, rich finishes, and elaborate molding. Look for classical motifs—columns, pediments, festooning, and acanthus leaves—for furniture details and accessories. Choose earth-tone colors such as ochre, terra cotta, and umber; include gold and ivory, and use ruby for a strong accent. Renaissance inspiration comes through in the rich colors and textures of textiles. Turn to classical values of balance and symmetry to provide cohesion.

sumptuous surroundings

Use layers of richness to establish a room: Overlay patterned sheer curtains with heavier ones in fringed chenille formed into ornate goblet pleats; bring together classical themes—a column-base lamp, and bronze- and verdigris-finished urns.

keys to successful style

1 Comfort is important to a style that values contented living; a large sofa provides ease. Choosing one with a pleated skirt adds elegance. 2 Select lamps with classical stature that comes from motifs such as urn shapes. 3 Look for rich Italian styling—strong molding, graceful scrolls, generous beading, contrasting veneers—in important pieces such as beds. 4 Ornately detailed boxes provide an impression of antiques. 5 Portraits bring to mind the Renaissance appreciation of artists. 6 An oversize, lavishly carved chair makes a regal impression with its bold pattern. 7 Bold furniture such as this oval drum table has an Old World richness.

1

2

3

4

5

6

7

Sumptuous upholstery in ochre and umber has a Renaissance quality.

Wrought iron supplies a rustic quality, here in classic arabesques.

Opulent finishes: warm wood tones, hand-painted florals, ornate metal pulls.

Textures—patterned sheers, fringed chenille, a carved-wood stay—add drama.

swedish country

Soft light drifting through cotton curtains and illuminating

the beauty of white formal furniture and fresh toile de Jouy

patterns; rooms that feel positively angelic in their grace

and calm—that's Swedish style at its best. Drawn to this

look are those who appreciate mid-1700s French styling yet

prefer a lighter, more casual approach. The result: a style

that's still highly refined—yet also exceedingly poetic.

the total effect

A Swedish look depends on completeness of background to carry off a serene refinement: Walls need to be a light color such as a linen tone; simple draperies are typically sweetly composed; accessories should be minimal and light—a glass cloche and a piece of coral allow light to move through them.

In Swedish style, it's easy to identify classic French Versailles furniture influences—and easier still to recognize that the pieces are transformed: lighter and purer in presentation and function, creating a distinct new beauty. Although the style began for the court of Sweden's King Gustav III, today one of its more appealing presentations is in Swedish Country.

Swedish Country is about:

- an overall feeling of airiness, and a generous use of snowy white;

- the classicism of Louis XVI furniture with its symmetry and straight lines, with an occasional Louis XV rococo design;

- wood furniture in natural tones or painted in tones of white;

- fabric coloring that pairs white with other colors such as blue, rose, black, lavender, or cream;

- upholstery patterns that include toile de Jouy, checks, and stripes;

- white curtains in a lightweight or sheer material, with the simplest treatments;

- the finish: crystal chandeliers, classical motifs, and blue and white ceramics.

climate of cultivation

Strategic styling pulls the look together: show upholstered chairs at their best by using two patterns of the same color to create additional interest; include gilded accents to add warmth; bring in a country feeling as subtly as possible—here, beadboard is applied to the walls. Design note: Eighteenth century Swedish wooden floors had wide planks in natural tones; today's updates can include a thin wash of white for a light though not pristine effect.

Swedish style is often referred to as Gustavian, after King Gustav III, who took over the throne in 1771 at the age of twenty-five. Ardently international in his thinking, he brought back with him from a tour of Versailles a desire to establish equal greatness in Sweden. He became an unfailing patron of the arts, creating an artistic golden age in Sweden. Furniture during his reign was mostly influenced by Neoclassical, Louis XVI, or Directoire periods; Gustav III incorporated influences from France and Italy by bringing architects and artists from those countries to his realm, as well as by sending Swedes to those lands for study. The Gustavian era continued until 1810. Two more Neoclassical styles—Empire followed by Biedermeier—ruled through 1850.

country styling

Swedish country improvises, differing from the classic approach, by including French Provincial and country influences, evident in the wheat-back chairs, chandelier, upholstered chair and ottoman, and wood mantel. Into this elegantly serene theme, incorporate herb plants and topiaries to discreetly add soothing color plus vitality.

Fabrics are an important part of the freshness of Swedish style, and no pattern establishes the look as effectively as toile de Jouy with its detailed outdoor scenes.

Near Versailles in 1760, a German-born textile printer named Christophe-Philippe Oberkampf responded to France's enthusiasm for the printed cottons that had recently come from India. In the town of Jouy, using copper plates, he worked on perfecting colorfast engravings on cotton, silk, and linen. The scenes in his fabrics were historical, pastoral, or seasonal. Once King Louis XVI was presented with the fabrics, they became a favorite of the court. Because of the extraordinarily high quality of the prints, toile de Jouy ("toile" is French for linen) remains the reference for excellent cloths in this patterning.

dream designs

Like other rooms in the house, Swedish country bedrooms are lightly furnished to create an airy quality. Accessories include sconces, mirrors, simple white curtains, and period-style lamps such as this gilded tole style. One beautiful presentation of toile for the bed is to contrast it with stripes and checks, adding double bed skirts such as this one with a crotcheted panel. Beneath the duvet, linens underline the Swedish theme of elegant white.

how to create
the look

Swedish style is about a light, white look that's open and airy. Furniture is Louis XVI-inspired with neo-classicism's straight lines, and is painted white. In Swedish Country rooms, toile de Jouy patterns are the fabrics of choice, paired with stripes and checks for added interest. Floors are bare or can be given a wash of white. Here, crystal chandeliers, classical motifs, mirrors with subdued frames, and black-and-gold accents provide finish.

remarkable romance

Mirrors need frames that are muted, such as the weathered look of this Adam-style mirror with its classic urn and valance motif. In the Gustavian era, rectangular gilt wood mirrors with this same motif were highly coveted.

keys to successful style

1 In a rubbed white finish, even a large piece such as this hand-painted bombé chest has a more intimate scale. 2 Louis XVI-inspired furniture is the backbone of Swedish style, with its straight, symmetrical styling, and lack of flourishes. 3 Occasional accents influenced by the Louis XV period, with its curves, add softness. Sconces bring eighteenth-century interest. 4 A white-painted panel bed establishes Swedish style in the bedroom and introduces a country mood. 5 A settee, rather than a sofa, establishes a living room, most effectively in a classic toile. 6 Gilded tole accessories recall the French 1760s 7 Country-inspired furniture, such as French Provincial-style chairs, and casual wood finishes, such as the whitewash on this table, can define Swedish Country in a dining room.

1

2

3

4

5

6

7

Black and white gain added interest in ticking stripes and crochet.

Sheer floral curtains filter light and complement a delicate rosemary plant.

With its rich black background, this toile de Jouy pattern makes an impact.

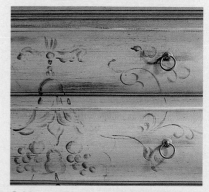

Subtle hand painting brings light, delicate design to white pieces.

british travel

The South Seas, India, Africa—the eighteenth and nineteenth centuries took the British officer to far-off, exotic points of adventure. And as English design met distant cultures, a new style naturally evolved. This is a look for someone who values classic English design coupled with rich, exotic influences, who desires a relaxed formality that brings distant destinations to your front door.

travel itinerary

In British Travel, one piece of furniture can have a variety of influences, as in this dressing stand and bureau (a style also recreated as British campaign furniture, gaining local impact after arrival). At first glance, it's Victorian, but the deeply fluted pilasters, whimsical caps on the feet, and hammered hardware capture the Caribbean.

One striking characteristic of British Travel is its ability to telegraph unusual and exotic locations without requiring a full-blown setting. Instead, in classic British tradition, there's strong understatement.

To express British Travel:

- Bring together beautiful eighteenth century formal English furnishings and accompany them with a few Victorian and American pieces.

- Look for captivating, varied influences on one piece of furniture, such as a coming together of Caribbean and Victorian.

- Include furniture whose deep or pronounced carving is one of its most riveting features, bringing in an exotic note.

Giving the look its intriguing sense of journey is an unusual complement of textures. Apply grass cloth to walls to add an exotic feeling, or, as shown here, use paint techniques to achieve the look. That same natural-fiber theme continues in the draperies which, although they have a classic box-pleat valance, are rendered in linen and finished in a fringed trim.

spice routes

Turn to a palette of khaki plus rich color—here it's paprika red—to invoke novel travel. Contrast a pattern, such as the exotic peacock motif on the duvet, with stripes for a mark of interest. With a touch as subtle as fan-shape lace trim, a Victorian influence rounds out the room. A motif resembling the wings of a tropical bird carved onto the headboard of the bed makes a rich contrast to a classic-style lamp.

A fascinating offshoot of the British campaigns was the creation of "knockdown" campaign furniture. It's an intriguing, absorbing glimpse into the talented minds of men who could dismantle furniture with the intricacy of watchmakers, reduce it to the fewest pieces, envision a compact, self-containing travel shape, and formulate the easiest reassembly.

As British gentlemen abroad filled the ranks of the government and military, they requested that refined furniture from home accompany them. Thus, some of the greatest furniture makers of the time—such as Chippendale and Hepplewhite—complied. Exact reproductions of furniture at the height of English style were made. Furniture designed for the campaigns is often recognizable by rectangular brass corners and handles. The production of campaign furniture continued through the Victorian age.

destination designs

British Travel style requires a layer of luxury to soften the commanding lines of the furniture. Bring in pillows in unusual patterns, keeping them in the same tones for unity. Add throws in rich designs to sofas and chairs. Enrich the room with deeply hued carpets. To give draperies extra design interest, choose natural fabrics and simple details such as a contrasting band.

97

how to create
the look

This style provides a beautiful look at English 1700s and Victorian furniture, telling a rich story of travel. Turn to classics in warm, deep wood tones with striking carving, as well as furniture where one piece shows varied influences. Bring in American Empire (the bedroom armoire) and Island or Anglo-India inspired pieces (the coffee table) for a well-rounded effect. Add atmosphere with natural materials such as linen draperies. Khaki is the base, along with an exotic color partner to maintain refinement.

richness of tones

The room should give the impression of a journey log of notable impressions. Beds make the most impact; look at the deep rope carving of this one, as Federal as it is Caribbean in feeling.

keys to successful style

1 An English-style sofa establishes the central theme of the look. **2** Attributes such as caning and legs that are detailed in an Anglo-Indian style can instantly introduce a sense of travel. **3** A Victorian dressing mirror was one of many pieces that could be designed as campaign furniture. **4** Anchor the look with accessories in classic styles such as lamps. **5** A bench gains rich character with horizontal carving and the English presence of heavy brass casters. **6** Beds should make a strong statement with notable, intricate carving. **7** Choose art that furthers the travel motif, as with reproductions of antique maps.

1

2   3

4   5

6   7

the palette

Choose khaki and paprika red tones, and pair exotic patterns with stripes.

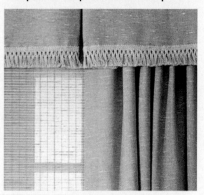

Natural textures make a background that suggests the Caribbean.

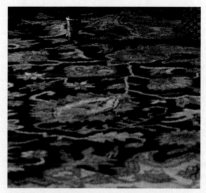

Deeply hued carpets give the impression of being acquired with travel.

Carved and beaded detailing establish a cultured, distinguished approach.

euro eclectic

It's as if you turned off the Champs-Élysées in Paris and entered your third-floor apartment. Or took the lift up to your flat at London's Sloane Square. Inside is a rich world that reflects you—no matter where you live: There's an appreciation for engaging diversity; a cultivated and energetic joining of European classics; a bright and unique styling that shows experience and sophistication—plus regard for elegant comfort. It's as if you're home.

elegant thought

In the European manner of overlooking the labels of rooms, the owner passed over a far-off study to transform an appealing sunroom off the bedroom into an office, with a classic European-style desk and a Louis XVI-inspired oval back chair. Instead of a wall of paintings, the confident and unusual choice is two exquisite hand-painted wall plaques. A Roman shade adds casual warmth.

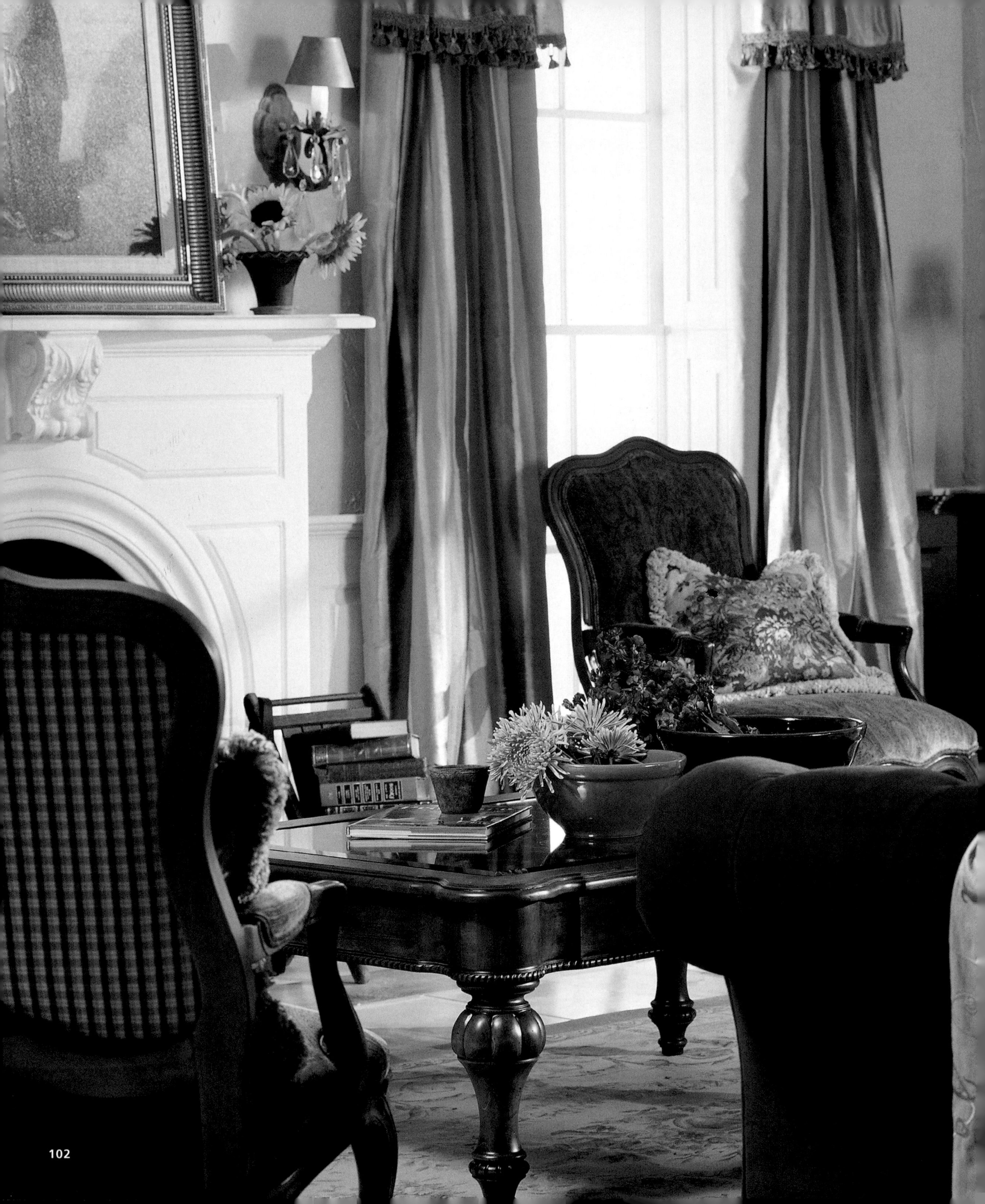

Giving a home that's filled with commanding pieces a bright and comfortable quality—rather than a starched, somber mood—is what these rooms are about, reflecting complete beauty and ease.

There's an appreciation for history in the choice of central pieces that allows interesting contrasts: England's graceful Georgian curves (the table) standing beside Regency neo-classicism (the chest); France's curving Louis XV rococo (the chairs) with more classical European-style (the desk) and Empire's dignity (the bed). To reproduce this look:

- Contrast a richly colored upholstered piece with the finishes of the wood furniture.

- Give curtains an easier approach. Rather than intricate and heavy swags and tails, a modern-feeling striped silk is casually gathered over a rod.

- Avoid a stuffy effect by painting walls a golden yellow —conveying a warm and interesting personality.

- Bring in accessories that show polish: the silk throw, the enticing stacks of leather-bound books within easy reach.

rich reception

Although every piece has an air of significance, at every turn there is a light note. Into the refinement of the Louis XV-style chairs and Georgian-style table comes a bold and plush red scroll-arm sofa. Making a corner convivial are the joyful red floral prints and beaded lampshade whose style is well supported by the serious Regency-style chest. While an Aubusson-style carpet carries importance, casual furniture placement announces confident, sociable ease.

The freshness of these rooms is what makes them feel exclusive. Often, period rooms have excessive weight—the outcome of a saturation of one period, in one wood tone, with traditional style approaches.

Here, the result of bringing a more worldly, lighter approach is still elegant, but uniquely so. For instance, pushing wicker storage baskets under the Empire-style bed doesn't diminish the bed's grand style, it strengthens its intimacy and plays up the warm honey tones and graceful lines. Instead of disharmony, combining an Empire-style bed with a Louis XVI-style chair, and introducing French Provincial-style dining pieces, creates novel charm in a small, open living space. Adding the unusual choice of red accents—the sofa, the glass goblets—into this neutral environment doesn't dilute the pedigree of the surrounding furnishings, it brings a wider and richer perspective to them.

demonstrative ways

A level of gentility shows up in the choice of flooring. The large-scale natural-and-cream-stenciled checkerboard echoes regal entryways as much as it does simple country floor treatments. The use of hand-painted tiles in the office is a nod to the stone floors of grand eighteenth-century homes, creating a distinct look for the room. In the bedroom, a period touch: As in the 1740s, molding is added to the wall, with wallpaper applied inside the panels, here in a later-period print.

how to create
the look

A luxurious, worldly approach is the framework for this eclectic look, bringing together a diversity of styles and periods. Putting that mix into a rich, bright environment means unique accompaniments, such as unusual treatments for windows, studied attention to flooring, and unexpected accent pieces. Informal additions such as vibrant, country-yellow walls establish a warm personality. The final result should be a home filled with classics that is as sophisticated as it is approachable.

elegance revisited

Gold, beige, and ochre unite elegant pieces as diverse as a Louis XVI-style secretary and Louis XV-style armchair, the layered window treatment and the checkerboard floor—notable for its oversized scale.

keys to successful style

1 A tufted sofa reflects the era's penchant for curves, and is scaled to hold its own with large pieces. In red, it's a confident surprise.   2 Art is rethought to include two panels—interpretations of a French folding screen—in place of paintings.   3 In a room where overall mood is the goal, the rug should have a fine degree of detail, giving it impressive but not overpowering interest.   4 A Victorian-style lamp with a beaded shade shows self-assured whimsy.   5 A collection of antique-inspired pillows signals regard for comfort in every room.   6 These Louis XV-style armchairs are included for fresh, updated styling that's free of excessive ornamentation.   7 A chest can make a serious statement and anchor a space. This one, in an unusual black and cherry finish, provides a grand note.

the palette

1

2

3

4

5

6

7

Striped silk pulls together the gold, sage, and ochre tones in the rooms.

A carpet in the style of Aubusson, a French village, lends a tapestry effect.

In the bedroom, pillows include rose and sage tones, with antique appeal.

A toile pattern, in gold and rose, brings elegance to a casual Roman shade.

107

contemporary living

distinctly modern

A large round mirror suspended low like a rising sun. A concentration of lavender turning fabrics into something sensuous. A geometric pattern conjuring a specific point in time.

Contemporary rooms have the ability to generate a stunning energy that's all their own. And without fail, these are rooms that are sleek and light-filled and feel gloriously spacious.

Yet there is no one look of contemporary. As seen on the following pages, contemporary style can range from influences as varied as country, Asian, cosmopolitan-formal, industrial, and retro. And pulling every look together is one overriding theme: the liberating quality of open, airy spaces—allowing fresh style to be on full view.

urban country

Friends dropping by, pets roaming freely, windows wide open and music on the stereo—"outgoing" describes this contemporary home. Furnishings have simple shapes, inspired by American Shaker and Arts and Crafts styles —with a modern twist that's meant to surprise. It's the lifestyle for someone who has a vivacious energy and a winning frankness—it's the country side of urban style.

drawing the line

The tall, strong lines of this Shaker-inspired bed take on drama in black and the addition of canopy rails brings balance to the bed and the room. The leather ottoman is a contemporary counterpoint to the Shaker-style side table. Framed by the bed, a pair of sepia-tone photographs becomes the focus of the room.

Urban country is as free-thinking as it sounds. The city quality comes from bold and contemporary furniture choices; from modern art and accessories; and from the high-energy atmosphere. The country aspect is solidly centered in the rural simplicity of American Shaker-style furniture. Because a spare style can sometimes feel cold, strategic design how-tos come into play, keeping the feeling warm:

- Choose an inviting color scheme; here it's neutrals enlivened with red, white, and blue.

- Include a few furnishings in accentuating colors, such as the light blue sofa and black bed.

- Ground the spaces with naturally hued carpets and bring in nature in unobtrusive ways with simple, unfussy plants.

- Add a variety of textures: the leather on the side table; the suede-like feel of the sofa; the tight weave of the rug; and the stitched-together quilting in the bedroom.

Additional interest comes from originality—rippled metal is used as a fireplace surround, extending to the ceiling. The rippled metal accomplishes two things: supplying an unexpected industrial element, and bringing in an engaging rustic barn quality.

artistic advances

The upside of modern furnishings can also be a dilemma: Furniture stripped of adornment is wonderfully sleek, but that simplicity can sometimes come off as flat. Filling that void, modern art brings a dynamic quality that can take center stage in this setting; here, energy derives from a colorful flag rendition. Smooth, rather than sleek, describes the contemporary club styling of the sofa and chair, the clean-lined Shaker-style table, and the leather trunk. Design note: Contemporary fireplace styling is often asymmetric and mantel-free.

The look shown here is achieved with a balance of Shaker and Arts and Crafts furniture styles. Making them modern is the neutral palette and the minimal use of accessories.

American Shaker furniture was at its height between the 1820s and 1850s. The Shakers (who had settlements throughout much of the east and in parts of the midwest) strove for simple, self-sustaining rural living, believing that their work and what they built expressed an inner spirit and religious experience. Shaker-style furniture has the innate beauty of functional, forthright designs that are free of ornamentation, and was built with superb craftsmanship—labors of modesty and utility that seem modern today.

Similarly, Arts and Crafts furniture, from the late 1800s to 1920s, also displayed simple lines, solid shapes, and visible joinery.

a blend of the best

Because Arts and Crafts inspired furniture can look heavy when combined with other styles, balance is key. A classic Shaker style table has perfect proportions for Arts and Crafts-style slat-back chairs; an Arts and Crafts-style sideboard and tall curio cabinet add balance across the room. In the dining room, two ingenious moves: a rug that has a quilted pattern; and metal used as wainscoting.

how to create
the look

Simplicity and careful combinations are the secrets to urban country. The simple, rural style of Shaker-style furniture is blended with the more massive feeling of Arts of Crafts. The palette is predominantly neutral, warmed with bursts of color in accessories or dramatic art. Urban statements come across in contemporary club furniture as well as in metal accents. A variety of textures—wovens, leathers—adds depth to the smooth, bold furniture shapes.

simple drama

For a variation on the urban country theme, try an oversized wall clock and bold fabrics to lend a contemporary edge. A traditional black wrought iron lamp can work as well as a modern one when its lines are this clean and its color echoes the ebony finish of the furniture.

keys to successful style

1 An Arts and Crafts-inspired curio cabinet provides a dramatic focal point in the dining room. 2 An upholstered club chair combines contemporary lines and softness, in off-white for a lighter look, with contrasting piping to trace its contours. 3 Art is an effective way to pull in country themes. Here, sepia-toned photographs of barns bring rural terrain inside. 4 An Arts and Crafts-style clock is updated in modern materials —an iron casing and a copper face. 5 An eminently useful Shaker-style side table can easily take on contemporary flair when one of its colors is sleek black. 6 The simple but dramatic lines of a Shaker-style pencil-post bed become more powerful in black with a geometric canopy.

1

2

3

4

5

6

In pale khaki and denim, these bedcoverings update classic country ticking patterns.

Patriotic colors, a mix of textures, and country whip stitching add warmth.

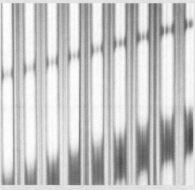

Corrugated metal, with its rural reference, becomes a modern element.

A rug combines the crisp look of a sisal with the softness of a Berber.

penthouse
view

Delightfully sophisticated—that's the view, start to finish.

This look speaks to anyone who takes pleasure in being

enveloped in a tailored, formal glamour, who's drawn to a

dramatic mix—such as contemporary pieces mingling with

classic furniture; Art Deco's glint and flair coming together

with classical art. Urbane and cosmopolitan, contemporary

and exciting—it is, put simply, the top.

curvaceous lines

How to make a mix of furniture
unite for this dramatic look:
choose pieces with the sleekest
curves. Here it's done with
contemporary pieces: the
Directoire-esque bed with its
streamlined design; the table's
Art Deco-style legs supporting a
top with classic valance fluting;
the dresser, with its concave
lines, mixing neoclassical and
French Deco styles. Bare floors
are buffed to a gloss.

Just out of frame could be a woman in a glittering evening gown that ends in a liquid-like train in back; a man in white-tie and tails, looking for his gloves and cane before they dash. That era of ravishing elegance and Hollywood-esque glamour fills these rooms, but it's held in check by a contemporary sensibility. To build the effect:

- start with white—in white and off-white upholstery, tables, and accessories, giving it the glamour-quotient that black has today;

- choose Art Deco influences to lend dynamic and streamlined polish: A sofa and chairs, in contemporary club styling, show these influences in the way their arms gently curve downward, in the clean bends of their wide design;

- introduce Art Moderne (early, modern-design 1920s furniture) styling to provide period panache—such as in a curved, platinum-finished, open-design table.

One piece of art should have a bigger-than-life quality, fulfilling the goal of all-out glamour: here, it's represented in an oversize hand-embellished print, classic in content, attention-getting in a gilded frame, standing insouciantly on the floor as a newest arrival.

cosmopolitan company

Acquiring an air of cultivation is, practically speaking, easy. It comes from the Georgian-style secretary and the George III-influenced ball-and-claw foot chair, and the impression that eighteenth century–style pieces are part of a family tradition, handed down and easily enfolded—quite smartly—into this very current mix.

Élan—a suave, 1930s-sounding word for
self-confident, highly fashionable style—
and these rooms have it. Although period
or club pieces could have succeeded here,
what elevates the room to full glamour
is its more interesting choice: formal
eighteenth-century shapes—the Directoire-
style table with its fine reeding; the round-
back comtemporized Adam-style chairs; the
Hepplewhite-inspired demilune console—
that have received sleek contemporary
styling, with cherry tones and burl finishes
contributing sophistication.

Self-assurance is evident in the pairing of
contemporary and classic furniture and
art—and by the unstudied display of art:
propped and stacked, their casual positioning inadvertently perfect. Success in these
rooms is achieved when nothing seems out
to impress; this elegance should appear to
have fallen spontaneously into place.

making arrangements

A serene background is a must for these glamorous furnishings or the full effect would be overpowering. Walls are saved from severity by fine
moldings and contrasting white paint treatments.
Adding to the lightness: draperies are unobtrusive
sheers; art has the muted tones of classical
anatomical line drawings. Silver and brushed
metal simultaneously continue Art Deco and
contemporary influences.

how to create
the look

Pairing formal with contemporary pieces is the start to this glamorous look: choose tailored pieces; turn to Art Deco influences to add the glitz—and curves— to contemporary club styling and accessories; add in classic eighteenth century-style pieces to establish a contrasting seriousness. Choose white for high style: in upholstery, tables, amply matted art, draperies, and walls that are molded and painted to add calm depth. Classical themes and shapes should dictate art and accessories.

the glamour of white

White—the color that was once the height of sophistication—is once again. Its effect of pure elegance comes from its three-dimensional layering—such as the white wall, table, lampshade and chair.

keys to successful style

1 The elegance of this Directoire-inspired bed comes from its contemporary sleekness and rich dark tones. 2 Contemporary and classic anatomical studies demonstrate the two style themes at work. 3 An eighteenth century Georgian-style secretary adds the balance of height to furniture whose contemporary forms are by nature low in profile.
4 Art Deco inspiration appears in this beautiful concave bowfront dresser with envelope detailing, the grain of the veneers is displayed both vertically and horizontally. 5 Classic urn shaping and a brushed-silver finish make this lamp ideal for a room of 1930s and contemporary styling. 6 Art Deco influence brings glamorous curves to a variety— rather than a matched set—of contemporary club chairs.

the palette

1

2

3

4

5

6

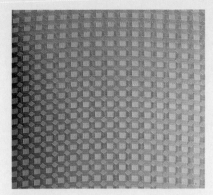

The tone-on-tone weave of a club chair's fabric has a glamorous, light sheen.

Blue and ecru damask adds subtle color and texture to a room of neutral tones.

A range of white and cream hues lends depth and contrast to the walls.

The shimmer of pale blue bedcoverings adds elegant contrast to deep wood tones.

loft living

This downtown loft is an urban utopia, outfitted with sleek style. But loft living isn't reserved for city dwellers—any room or space can serve as a loft, it just takes the right design elements and point of view. So if the prospect of an urban perspective and an airy, expansive-feeling space with few walls feels energizing, then the pleasures of loft living are ideal. It's a modern meeting of the minds for fashion and function.

strong silhouettes

Because of the openness of the space, each piece of furniture receives artful regard, so choose pieces with a sculptural quality. White is the classic loft paint choice, serving as a canvas for these furnishings. Instead of walls, partitions define—rather than separate—rooms, keeping this bedroom connected to the larger space.

Loft designers report that defining the needs of the space is always the first step. This loft is divided into three sections: living, dining, and sleeping. Loft living is defined by:

- the openness of the space;

- multitasking areas and multifunctional pieces;

- pieces with strong lines;

- furniture that, because of the open space, is pleasing to view from 360 degrees;

- a high level of organization that rules out clutter;

- furniture in sync with the scale of the space—fifteen-foot-high ceilings can accommodate oversized furniture, while a traditional ceiling height is best with low-scale pieces.

Although just about any style can work in a loft, contemporary/modern is particularly effective because of its dynamic yet clean and architectural lines. The city-roots appeal of the living room shows up in the geometric lines of the sofa and in sleek furnishings. The floor lamp was selected for its sculptural and transparent styling.

red hot

Intense, consistent color works in a loft because it's diffused by the airiness of the space, and makes each piece seem unique. Red doesn't just grab attention, it makes everything around it stand out as well: The white background becomes pristine, silver frames and metals shimmer, and the magnetic focal point of the room isn't a major upholstered piece but a single cobalt blue bowl. The white Berber carpeting adds tailored softness.

The multifunctional aspect of loft living is what sets it apart. The living and dining rooms are relaxing enough for comfortable down-time, stylish enough for entertaining, and can be rearranged to support a variety of activities: Spread out paperwork at the ample kitchen table one night, host a dinner party the next. Roll kitchen chairs to each room for extra seating as the evening dictates. In the bedroom, a desk carves out space for a stylish and private home office; it can be lifted into the entertaining areas when an extra table is required for larger get-togethers.

Since everything is on full view in a loft, consistent storage containers—such as the red boxes here—wind up becoming part of the style message. The same balance is seen in the bookcase, where, to keep the open look, storage and books are placed rather than packed. In the living room, the openness of the bookshelf serves as a fluid room divider.

supporting roles

Urban influences show up in the flooring as well as the furniture. White deck paint moves seamlessly to the white brick walls, allowing the furniture to seem to float and the space to feel larger. In the kitchen, durable industrial rubber flooring (also ideal in exercise spaces and bathrooms) adds a graphic effect through its raised texture.

133

how to create
the look

"Form" and "function" are the bywords of loft living. Most spaces in lofts are best defined with bookcases, half-walls, and screens. Each piece of furniture requires serious planning since not only is it on full display, but there's also a good chance it will do duty in several areas. Be strategic with color; here, red is consistent for upholstery, bedcoverings, and even storage. The overall impression is open, airy, and sleek.

open air

Unobstructed views around the room and "through" pieces, as well as the unhindered movement from one designated space to another, is what defines the concept of airiness. It's achieved with open-back bookcases that have artful, spare arrangements. It comes from chairs that have open arms and coffee tables with open shelves. And it's enhanced by transparent materials and light-reflecting metals.

keys to successful style

1 The clean geometric shape and contemporary styling of a sofa such as the Tribeca is the sculptural starting point.   **2** The standing lamp brings together two industrial materials—glass and metal—for framed transparency.   **3** Caster rollers on chairs reiterate the industrial influences.   **4** The elliptical coffee table reflects the curves that are hallmarks of much contemporary design.   **5** Wall décor that is overtly graphic offers a more modern presentation.   **6** Rather than a platform bed that rests on the floor, this contemporary style of bed allows air to flow all around. The duvet continues the red color theme, and its geometric plaid enhances the bed's architectural lines.   **7** An accent chair, like any additional piece, needs to make its own powerful graphic statement.

the palette

1

2

3

4

5

6

7

Strong colors make textural elements like metal and glass more prominent.

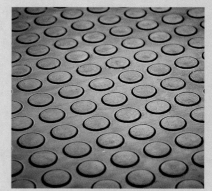

Touches of chrome can enhance the industrial feel of a space.

A unique, graphic flooring, industrial rubber tile comes in a variety of colors.

The combination of red and blue, purple makes an ideal design accent.

retro modern

It's a new kind of groovy—a look that's upbeat, nostalgic, high-style, and very, very livable. It's for the person who values midcentury design and exuberance yet doesn't want to live inside a time capsule—in fact, there's not one drop of kitsch in this home. And yet, with softer colors and styling, the mood is as open-minded and pleasure-giving as it ever was, because it's the newest way to live with the beauty of retro…today.

the new fluidity

Water, a central inspiration for many of the organic shapes in midcentury design, has a new role here: The aquatic palette makes for a more contemporary, calmer atmosphere, and relaxes even further the broad contours of the furnishings and accessories.

The 1940s, '50s, and '60s—midcentury decades—were some of the most exciting in modern design, inspiring many of today's modern looks. Architects began designing exhilarating furniture that was devotedly casual, with streamlined shapes meant for lounging. That ease is still present in new interpretations—in subtler ways.

Consider:

- upholstery that takes its cues from the past with appealing wovens and raised textures, but in solids rather than bright geometrics;

- furniture shapes that are soft rather than strictly geometric;

- coffee tables that are upholstered rather than planes of glass and metal;

- walls with soft color rather than white;

- accessories that still have flair but are more subdued, such as the retro geometric pillows.

Even floor treatments for this look have evolved. In the '60s and '70s, time spent socializing sitting on the floor led to softer rugs that got wild: fluffy white flokati rugs (woven rugs from Greece) and shag carpeting, either of which could overpower today's restrained approach. What works best is less self-conscious—a textural weave that provides the softness and dimension, but in a gentler, more modern way.

a stylish balance

Straightforward lines and roomy, upholstered comfort make the sofa a subtle standout. More interesting than a second sofa is the ample armchair, its proportions lending beautiful balance to the room. Whimsically shaped ottomans such as these are the coffee table of choice for this look.

Blond wood tones were beloved by American, European, and Scandinavian designers for their ability to give even large pieces of furniture a feeling of lightness, so it's no wonder that it's a favorite of contemporary designers, too. As stylish as the furniture is, it's also packed with practicality, evident in the bedside tables with multiple drawers, and in door chests that hold everything from clothing to stereos.

Here, light woods play up wonderfully frank shapes reminiscent of mid-century design: the easy curve of the bed, the clean lunar outline of the dining table, the sharp geometrics on the chairs, and the studiously simple detailing of classic tapered legs.

The infusion of fun, then and now, comes as much from shapes as from lively patterned fabrics. The midcentury was an era when textile designers were given high artistic regard. The era's spirited and lighthearted textiles for draperies, upholstery, linens, and pillows brought the furnishings to life.

full circle

Cheerful, retro-inspired textiles, on the bed and as a window treatment, pick up the soft aqua theme. Orange, a popular accent in days past and now, is the only accent color. Large tiles on key walls in the bedroom and dining room form graphic backdrops.

how to create
the look

Comfortable, relaxed, and jet-age sleek—that's what makes retro styling so desirable. Today's interpretation is softer. It's about roomy upholstered pieces mixed with blond woods in simple lines and geometrics. Colors—more muted than in the past—are used to create a calming mood. Choose accessories with tones of metals such as chrome and brushed stainless steel to reprise the automobile-inspired excitement of the era.

honest approach

Midcentury furniture celebrates, rather than attempting to hide, the function of a piece of furniture. Like much blond mid-century furniture, this light-color door chest is devoted to function while imparting a finely crafted elegance.

keys to successful style

1 A sofa with straightforward lines automatically opens a room and gives a modern message.   2 Let small pieces add the spin: Expressing post-war America's fascination with outer space, satellites, and robotics, this witty side table incorporates glass, metal, blond wood, and classic curves.   3 The strong curves, dips, and lines of the slat bed add to the graphic message.   4 Add vases that have curves—reminders of the biomorphic shapes of midcentury glassware.   5 Keep details sleek: Go with frames in silvery metal finishes.   6 Strongly graphic chairs bring visual interest to simple dining tables.   7 Choose ottomans in clean but unusual shapes to continue the modern theme; pull them close to serve as contemporary coffee tables.

1

2

3

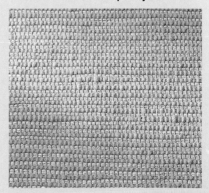

4

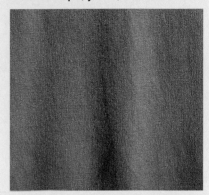

5

6

7

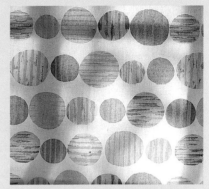

The retro-inspired pattern uses softer shades of aqua, yellow, and cream.

Orange returns as the friendly and exuberant burst of color for accents.

A cool background color adds depth and creates a more contemporary aesthetic.

Soft rugs with raised textures are today's practical response to shag carpeting.

zen palette

The gentle glow of a setting sun, the sensation of a breeze drifting inside through an open window, the textures of stones worn smooth by time…. Feelings of peace and pleasure, and a fuller connection with nature, can fill a home that's open to Eastern influences, rejuvenating the mind, body, and spirit. By introducing principles for harmony, interiors will easily resonate with this higher level of sophistication.

room for reflection

A large round mirror, rather than a rectangular one, creates harmonious balance—think of the sun, the moon. The mirror's low placement transforms the top of the bureau into the horizon line. Complementary shades of soft blue and golden saffron pull in the sky and sun.

Creating a haven from cell phones, faxes, and schedules begins with a complete concept:

- that less will be more;
- that airiness will be emphasized with soothing natural tones;
- that tactile pleasures will have precedence;
- that furniture, though simple, will carry exotic notes;
- that light will increase in importance;
- and that the desired outcome for design as well as atmosphere is a soothing balance.

The sophisticated feeling of the rooms comes from modern furniture that simply suggests the East. Dark, richly colored wood pieces bring to mind their exotic pedigrees: The simplicity of the bed is reminiscent of a Chinese daybed, with the headboard suggesting the form of a Japanese screen. Even the night table carries the mystery of a chest. How do you take this room to the next level of design know-how? By mixing in a choice few ultra-contemporary pieces, adding streamlined ease.

everyday enlightenment

The impact of light on mood makes it a significant part of the design of any room. Natural light is welcomed into this bedroom and treated as a design element, with a floor-to-ceiling open screen behind the bed that shifts light coming through the wall of windows. For more control over the amount of light in your room, try draperies in a translucent grid to repattern the light (as in the living room on the next page) or wooden blinds that allow every variation—from full morning sun to narrow stripes of afternoon light to evening privacy.

The inspirations for the restful mood as well as for the natural colors and materials here are basic elements such as wood, metal, earth, air, fire, and water.

The desire to touch comes from the collection of metals, silky fabrics, woven throws, textured pillows, and groupings of bamboo, stones, and vases with musical-instrument-like shapes. Dark woods suggest the earth, while pared-down upholstered furniture finds beauty in sand and moss colors. Red and ember-orange accents are spare: on books, in flowers, and on one wall. Water's inspiration shows up not just in color but in easy, fluid, unobstructed movement around the pieces.

The benefits of creating a tranquil home: harmony, balance, and enhanced energy —in oneself.

arrangement as art

Every decorative element is included because it's regarded as a beautiful object and part of a still life. That consideration is seen in the linear, spare presentation of plates in the cabinet; in the contemplative care given each component of the table setting; in the attentive balance of bed pillows; and in the thoughtful composition of vases.

how to create
the look

Serenity, simplicity, and fluidity can define every element of this sophisticated style. Furniture is pared down, not just in design but in content, to create more wide-open spaces. Natural tones, materials, and textures give the room sensory interest. Dark, exotic-toned woods anchor the spaces, while a few lighter, more frankly modern upholstered pieces or metals give the rooms a wider perspective. The mood is set by the abundance of natural light, by the controlled plays of color, and by the artful placement and balance of furniture and accessories.

beauty and balance

Suspended on wires, two earth-tone prints seem balanced in mid-air, breaking up the rhythmic lines of the wooden privacy blinds. Adding to the airy feeling of the room is the upholstered chair's armless design.

keys to successful style

1 Distilled to its basics: a sleek metal-based lamp with the textured interest of a ribbed shade to diffuse light.   2 As simple as a bench, the dark wood coffee table establishes a tranquil mood due to minimal accessories on both levels.   3 An uncomplicated white sofa adds to the airiness, while its wood base suggests an Asian influence.   4 Organic in shape, vases reflect the element of water.   5 The sculptural, fluid lines of this contemporary recliner encourage relaxation.   6 The rolling cabinet's glass shelves are practical, yet lend it a lightweight quality.

1

2

3

4

5

6

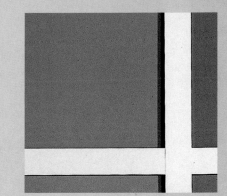

A grid pattern in soft grays creates a calm environment.

A single orange wall infuses the otherwise cool living room with excitement.

Bamboo reflects the Asian influence while adding exotic textural interest.

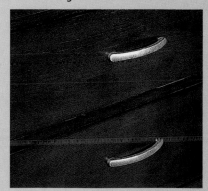

Dark finishes coupled with simple metals have a natural, rich attraction.

151

casual country

the joys of country

It's a look that begs to be enjoyed: Drop into the embrace of a plush armchair, and you feel immediately at home—wherever you are—with the overwhelming, pleasurable desire to stay put and enjoy.

The pleasures of country go straight to the heart: beautiful, open-hearted rooms; generous furniture intended for lingering; and an easy, feet-up freedom. All of these enjoyments can be found on the following pages, in lifestyles as varied as a modern approach, a sweet cottage, a rustic southwestern lodge, a first home, and a casual beach house. Every style is country-fresh, loosened up even further with new approaches.

And they all have one thing in common: an old-fashioned invitation to be yourself, as you indulge in these cozy and wonderfully comfortable rooms.

simple charm

The comfort of an old-fashioned iron-frame bed; buffet

lunches served from a trestle dining table; easy entertaining

in a bright, cheerful great room—these are the pleasures of

a light, simple way to live. The charm of this informal

country look is its subtle contemporary side, making it ideal

for city life—or for bringing a smart, urban sensibility

to the suburbs or the country. This clean look is instantly

easygoing, casually on-the-go—and engagingly sociable.

comfort and calm

The bedroom's feeling of sanctu-
ary comes from the soothing
spareness of a country room that
isn't overdecorated, allowing
appreciation for the bed—a cur-
vaceous, classic hoop bed with
simple styling, whimsical detailing, and restful bedcoverings.
A sleek contemporary lamp keeps
the look fresh.

At the heart of this look: lifestyle. It's about an energetic, almost sporty approach to living, with the belief that the more open the house is, the more open the lives inside will be; the less cluttered the rooms, the more freedom of movement. This look is about:

- roomy, unimposing furniture such as a wing back chair and classic long, curved-arm sofa;
- restrained country styling that includes contemporary pieces such as the sleek coffee table;
- unfussy upholstery to add a sleeker feeling;
- using baskets in bold, direct ways—for instance, as a side table—rather than as smaller, purely decorative elements.

In these rooms, there are overwhelming indications of a clear preference for filling the home with the interaction of family and friends rather than an overabundance of collected objects. The full charm of this stylish look comes from its ease and simplicity—two traits that are always key to country.

open minded living

With a great room—a combination of kitchen, dining room, and living room—the lack of walls allows light to move and air to flow unimpeded. Echoing that message are the open design of the coffee table and the cheery yellow paint that's subtle enough to give the illusion of a larger space. Instead of a bright carpet, this beige and teal woven makes a soft, smooth base; repeating it in the dining area connects the rooms.

Beauty, combined with smart practicality, always comes out ahead in the best of any country look—and here, it's what gives these rooms understated glamour.

Shaker furniture reflects both qualities, with its beautifully unadorned lines and practical design. The Shaker influence shows up in the dining room's trestle table, with an iron base that suggests the hand-forging of a blacksmith's shop; iron materials show up again in the early-American inspired chandelier.

Colorations are also Shaker inspired, from warm, natural wood tones to understated teals, butter, and biscuit tones. Accessories are unassuming as well, with milky-white vases or pale-yellow hand-thrown ceramics. Rather than a grouping of paintings, one oversize clock resembling a vintage store clock adds appeal; hung low and over a buffet console, it's placed like a work of art.

functional comfort

Although the lines of the furniture are simple, a second look shows a deeper level. Graphic dining chairs add a contemporary, confident energy to the space. Upholstery gains interest in raised crewel work or in a soft toile, with accent pillows gently repeating the tones. The lack of embellishment also comes through in unadorned windows that maximize light and contribute to the clean-lined look.

how to create
the look

This home gets its charm from comfortable furniture that has simple, Shaker-inspired silhouettes. Chairs and sofas have a straightforward, tailored appeal in soft and casual country tones of teal, biscuit, butter, and honey. Wood pieces have rich honey tones and are often paired with black iron for a more rustic effect. A few contemporary pieces, such as the glass-top coffee table, invigorate the country styling. Keeping the look open: a clean approach, from sleek lighting to a few simple but effective accessories.

a way with light

A light touch moves throughout the rooms. Beyond the gentle colors, it's in the raised, tone-on-tone design of the chair and pillow fabric, in the light-reflecting quality of the slim metal lamp base and sleek brushed-nickel cabinet pulls. The coffee table has a weightlessness that comes from the glass top and the muted gleam of brushed nickel finished legs.

keys to successful style

1 Although very country, the black-finished iron hoop bed has a contemporary feeling in its clean lines and lack of frills. 2 An elongated, nickel-tone finished lamp is a contemporary version of a table lantern. 3 This urban-style, glass-top coffee table has an openness that adds to the affable spirit of the home, while its size and surface are ideal for entertaining. 4 The simple lines of the sofa make it unobtrusive, while the buttery color adds country warmth. 5 Contemporary chairs with a graphic design bring fresh interest to a country dining room. 6 The Shaker-inspired wood and iron trestle table makes a practical and casually dramatic dining table. 7 Adding to the light, country appeal— hand-thrown ceramics in milky tones.

1

2

3

4

5

6

7

Soft florals and plaids in teal and peach create a restful country mood.

A chair's raised crewel work lends unobtrusive interest and texture.

In teal and cream, the woven rug grounds the room in a light, unfussy way.

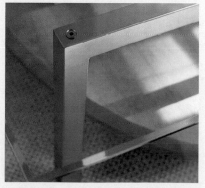

The coffee table's lightness comes from glass and brushed metal.

vintage mix

Romantic, breezy, and charming—vintage style has an unaffected warmth and presence that's irresistible. It's an ideal look for someone who loves an eclectic approach: mixing fabrics, pulling together different styles of furniture, and layering floral patterns. Slightly nostalgic in feeling, and full of garden accents and tea-stained fabrics, it's a quintessentially cozy and comfortable look.

spontaneous style

Vintage style should feel as if the pieces have been inherited or acquired over time and have, almost randomly, turned out to be perfect together. For instance, bistro chairs might not normally suit a fluted leg table, but in this open and airy room, where collected pieces are the norm, it's a perfect—and original—match.

Vintage style has the feeling of a favorite sweater you've worn forever. It feels familiar, stylish, and soothing in an understated way. The look is defined by:

- floral fabrics, some bright, some with a tea-stained effect, others vintage or vintage-inspired;

- furniture with different pedigrees—such as the Swedish-style arch-top bookcase and cabinet; the fluted leg table; the tufted Victorian-style armchair; and American nineteenth century-style bed;

- garden furniture, such as the bistro chairs, and outdoor motifs making a strong presence in everything from accessories to fresh flower cuttings;

- a white background for the rooms and the furniture, making a clean, clear base;

- a palette of muted rose and cream tones, along with stronger injections of rose color;

- a layering of fabric—florals, checks, and stripes—providing a homey feeling;

- the use of slipcovers and detailed pillows and cushions for chairs and sofas;

- period elements such as sconces and beadboard walls.

The friendliness of the look comes from the fact that there's nothing precious or overly delicate about the pieces—nothing has to be tiptoed around. As a result, there's an automatic sense of "I belong here" that's felt by everyone who enters the room.

in terms of white

Layering pulls the room together in several ways. First, white-on-white makes a serene, elegant background on the far wall even though there is a lot of detail there to occupy the eye. Second, details are layered for an intriguing appearance: ropes of beads on sconces; ruching on the curved back of the sofa; sweet strips of trim on the pillows; and the crisp piping and ties on the checked cushion.

167

While this look is wonderfully sophisticated, its charm comes unexpectedly from a slightly unfinished, casual effect. For instance, the beadboard paneling is most effective left slightly distressed, with just a wash of color. The still lifes look as if they just happened to fall together, with none of the self-conscious formality of eighteenth century European tableaux. The effect of the intentionally unmatched fabrics—particularly for pillows and throws—adds to the sincere styling.

Contributing to the unpretentious feeling of the rooms is the palette, with muted, soft roses in florals and toile de Jouy, along with antique creams and whites that have quaint handkerchief trim.

timeless appeal

The sentimental feeling of the look is a powerful draw. Enhance it with vintage fabrics or with beautiful reproductions such as these to cross the boundaries of "present" and "past". Bring in vintage-feeling furniture as well, such as pieces with cut-outs or turned posts, or with endearing carvings.

POPPIES

PANSIES

SNAPDRAGONS

Gardens go hand in hand with the vintage look. How do they mesh? Extend the same palette—muted corals and soft creams—outdoors. Select furniture that is designed to withstand the elements and also has the feeling of indoor pieces, such as this wicker-look collection. Accessorize as you would indoors by bringing out pillows and throws in a variety of patterns and textures, and by using your prettiest linens. Finally, make greenery one of your most important accessories. Use interesting cache-pots wherever you can, and set out vases of cut flowers.

garden grandeur

To incorporate the outdoors into a vintage look, treat every element as if it's an extension of the indoors. Here, the garden gate is given a cottage-style design and hardware, with the muted paint color tying directly into the palette. Likewise, the flower-filled urn receives the attention of a dining-room table centerpiece, adding natural sophistication.

171

how to create
the look

The charm of vintage style comes from its unpretentious sophistication and its emphasis on unmatched styling. Choose fabrics in muted colors and floral themes, stripes, and checks. Bring together furniture with different styling, such as French Provincial, American Colonial, and Swedish. Rely on white to make a clear background for nostalgic colors. Look for fabric details such as ruching and intricate trims.

romantic sophistication

A corner contains all the elements of vintage style: upholstery, color, and pattern themes on the tufted, floral Victorian-style arm chair; the white background and period detailing of a pressed-tin screen; the layering of a large and comfortable tea-stained pillow with a flounced ruffle. Rugs provide a warm finish.

keys to successful style

1 Transport garden furniture indoors; French-style bistro chairs have an airiness that contrasts with heavier furniture.   2 Choose light finishes for large pieces, allowing them to blend with the light, muted palette. 3 Floor clocks are best in white to maintain a lightweight quality; a Swedish-inspired case clock with a whitewashed finish brings exquisite detailing.   4 Rather than ornate or glass vases, turn to garden pots to combine the outdoors with the indoors.   5 Armchairs should have gentle lines and roomy design; look for contrasting piping and dressmaker box pleats for warm appeal.   6 Side tables should be unobtrusive; choose classic styling, such as this Sheraton-style candle stand.   7 The more personal-feeling the piece of furniture, the richer the effect of vintage style; a Country French-influenced writing desk has a sweetly detailed star carving.

1

2

3

4

5

6

7

Reproductions of vintage fabrics bring a timeless quality to the rooms.

Checks and stripes make a comfortable contrast to richly detailed florals.

Rugs beautifully replay the muted palette, especially in needlepoint motifs.

Mix floral patterns and rose and cream colors, layering them for effect.

ski lodge

High in the mountains of New Mexico, snowed in on a crystal-clear day, the beauty of lodge styling is readily apparent. This look appeals to someone who appreciates a streamlined, rustic environment, and is at home with bold, unfussy furniture and Western-inspired materials. It's the lifestyle for someone who values the outdoors, drawn to a relaxing retreat that's as sophisticated as it is country.

large scale

In lodge style, furniture is first and foremost generous in size and uncomplicated: Sofas should be long enough for napping; coffee tables large and sturdy enough for putting your feet up or accommodating casual dinners; side tables ample enough for gloves and mugs as well as a lamp; lounge chairs roomy enough for curling up with a blanket and book.

Lodge architecture has undergone a change. Before, sprawling nineteenth century lodges had significant impact on individual homes. So in the recent past, ski and mountain retreats resembled cabins more than chalets. They had rough-hewn beams; tree bark left on the timber; dark interiors with few windows; and more rooms with low ceilings than with cathedral ceilings. Today, the look is airier and smoother. Although natural wood and exposed beams are still the mainstay, the finish of the wood is smoother. Cathedral or taller-than-usual ceilings appear more frequently. There's a loft-like lack of separation between some of the rooms— a living room that flows into a dining area; a bedroom with a large sitting area, the sleeping area defined by a raised platform. Windows are extremely large to take in broader vistas.

country textures

In architecture and styling, textures are amazingly rich. The home's smooth, light-tone wood walls, beams, ceiling, and floor create a feeling of comfortable containment, and make a striking contrast to rough, exposed brick walls. When choosing furniture, emphasize contrasts: Wrought iron balances the wood of the rooms and furnishings; sophisticated leather treatments are made Western with nailhead trim. Include classic upholstered pieces for stately balance.

Lodge styling has a frank easiness that goes beyond the sporty element of the look. To get the handsome effect:

- choose furniture with strong, clean shapes, in generous sizes;

- update the style with a mix of furniture such as English Regency dining chairs, a French Provincial chandelier, a pencil post bed, and Mission side tables;

- be sure to include a range of Western textures such as leather, suede, denim, and fleece; kilim adds a global perspective;

- look for furniture that combines country materials, such as the dining table's wide planked wood top with a scroll-leg wrought iron bistro table;

- include accessories that play up this region: Native American blankets and fabrics, cowboy hats, vintage sports equipment, and cacti;

- keep carpets simple and neutral to blend with the wood of the floor and walls.

The palette is taken directly from nature: sky-blues, earth-tone tans, and wild-berry red.

bedroom with a view

In the loft-like layout of new lodge styling, the sleeping area must often be distinguished. Accomplishing this is a simple elevated platform that also provides a better view of the outdoors. Windows should be left unadorned or given a simple treatment to complete an open, sleek effect.

how to create
the look

Lodge style is defined by an outdoorsy outlook. It has straightforward, boldly shaped furniture and Western overtones. Choose pieces with an eye to comfort, going for ample shapes and selecting a range of styles. Look for furniture with Western inferences, such as nailhead trim and wrought iron. Put together a mix of country textures: leather, suede, wool, and denim in nature-inspired colors.

western exposure

Choose sturdy furniture that's free of excess detailing and has straightforward, accommodating shapes. Here, the open-back bookshelf is pure and simple, yet holds its own because of the thick lines of its design. Likewise, additional furnishings are more devoted to comfort than to making attention-getting statements.

keys to successful style

1 Bring in furniture in roomy shapes—this sofa has the luxurious texture of leather in a warm caramel brown.   2 Establish a mix of traditional and contemporary art, with nature as the theme.   3 Primitive-style clay pieces add a disarming purity to the idea of lodge art.
4 Have a selection of pillows available for use on the sofas and chairs as well as for lounging on the floor; kilim adds an international influence.   5 Look for furniture that combines country materials; this table has a planked wood top and wrought iron base.   6 Use muted tapestry fabrics for upholstery, giving pieces as basic as a club chair a presence that's as confident as it is country.   7 Arts and Craft-inspired mica lampshades call to mind the glory days of lodges and cast warm amber light.   8 Find details that transform a furnishing: Nailhead trim immediately gives a casual air to a leather dining chair.

1

2

3

4

5

6

7

8

Fleece and kilim textiles are used as upholstery, adding depth to the look.

This leather's earthy tan is the base of the home's warm, natural palette.

A mix of textures—leather, suede, and wovens—make a bed luxurious.

Kilims and Native American textiles contribute a handmade quality.

181

first home

You've waited a long time for this—the first home you can

completely call your own. And even on a budget, you want

it to have a look that's completely sophisticated. And this

is it: American classics you can build on, as your space and

budget evolve. The furnishings are comfortable, practical,

and have statement-making flair that everyone wants—

especially when it's for their beautiful beginning.

dual purpose

Because living space is probably less than generous, and a budget is less than large, opt for pieces that have dual uses: this drop-leaf side table can function all day as a hall table for keys and mail, and also perform as-needed in the role of a useful desk. An updated French-style bistro chair adds a whimsical note.

Particularly when you're taking the first step in home design, every piece of furniture has added significance. There's a natural need to feel the pride of making those first major design decisions, of having them work out— and watching the rooms come alive.

So when you're starting out:

- meet with a design consultant to make a detailed master plan and designate the first big-ticket pieces you need;

- consider the space you have; don't set your sights on oversize furniture if your residence is on the small side;

- bypass trendiness and go for classic shapes that you can build on and that can be used in other rooms later;

- work with an easy-to-achieve style, such as casual comfort;

- include dual-purpose furniture;

- create an airy effect: Having fewer pieces actually produces greater style.

surprising moves

Careful planning and decisions make these rooms interesting for their strategies as well as their designs. Here, a basic sectional has been recently partnered with another piece, forming an L that delivers greater lounging space than two sofas. The ottoman opens to reveal abundant storage capacity. In lieu of a large upholstered chair, a dining chair is invited in. In the bedroom, an antique-style pie safe, chosen for its narrow dimensions, makes an original and charming storage piece.

With their lasting elegance and comfortable composition, Windsor chairs are among the surest, most versatile furnishings to bring into any first home. The style's greatest characteristics are its arched, continuous back made from one piece of wood, and the spindles that connect it to a plank seat. The chairs were first introduced to the American colonies in 1754. A New England style developed that had one continuous piece of wood extending for the bow back and arms. Most large American cities soon began producing Windsors. Because several types of wood were used, the chairs were almost always painted, often green, black, red, or blue. The appeal of these sturdy classics with their airy quality and graceful design continues today.

color cues

Use color as a terrifically inexpensive design component for country style. Here, choosing black gives chairs eye-catching impact. Paint walls throughout a home to bring a caring attention to the spaces. An ideal way to go is with a subtle and elegant taupe, such as the one in this dining room, a soothing robin's-egg blue in the bedroom, and muted apple green in adjoining spaces, creating winning sophistication.

The Shakers typified the American character of inventiveness, not only with their beautifully simple furniture but also with their striving to create new ways to make their lives more productive. Among their liberating inventions are the fountain pen, circular saw, and fabric waterproofing techniques. One of their most well-known inventions is the flat broom—a development that created a steady source of income. Inventions such as these tied into the Shakers' faith: Greater work efficiency produced more time for their pursuit of spiritual and moral growth.

style signals

Three ways to create a polished look: classic furniture with American roots such as Shaker-inspired shapes; a neutral color base that provides steady sophistication, and easily changeable fabric accessories—here in cheerful red, white, and blue; a few pieces of large artwork, rather than clusters of small ones, to create a confident message of quality—unfilled wall space around them will attain a restful, rather than an unfinished, feeling.

how to create
the look

This is sophisticated style built around classic shapes such as the American pieces shown here, with an eye toward timelessness, practicality, and comfort. Choose pieces with dual functions to save floor space and budgets. Use sectional components that can be combined to create a larger piece or that can function independently. Color brings sophistication to furniture as well as walls. Choose a classic neutral for upholstered pieces, using accessories for color boosts.

linear perspective

Choosing one central pattern—here it's straight lines—and carrying it through creates a pulled together look that's easy to achieve. Selecting large pieces with character that have an open quality—such as the lamp and Windsor chairs—helps the room feel larger.

keys to successful style

1 Sectional upholstery with traditional styling is an ideal way to build up seating over time.   2 This upholstered ottoman has generous storage ability and also works as a bench and a table.   3 A wood and metal bistro chair brings strong styling and a touch of whimsy to any setting.   4 Include folk art, such as a hand-painted checkerboard that also functions decoratively.   5 This lamp's generous size, classic shape, and dark finish deliver an impressive statement.   6 Classic and sturdy, the popularity of this style of chair is unwavering.   7 This pharmacy style lamp with rustic finish, has a lean profile to maintain an airiness.   8 The pie safe is as at home in the dining room or kitchen as it is in the hallway.

the palette

1

2

3

4

5

6

7

8

Red, white, and blue add easy energy to rooms based on neutral tones.

Tailored rugs that pick up on fabric patterns complete this look.

The country theme comes across in patchwork motifs and soft stripes.

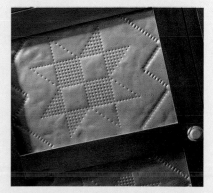

Pierced metal panels on a cabinet reproduce a country quilt motif.

beach house

The splash of the surf on the beach, cloudless blue skies

up above, and the soft crunch of sand under bare feet—

beach house living is one of life's greatest pleasures. And

it's the kind of lifestyle you can reproduce anywhere,

year-round. So if you enjoy a casual approach with white

furnishings and wicker, then you're already halfway

home—at the beach.

relaxed style

Comfort and lack of pretension are the nature of beach style. You can see it in furniture that's purely functional (open book shelves and open coffee tables for quick retrieval), in easy accessories (baskets for keeping essentials at hand, tightly woven rugs for simple cleaning), and in low-fuss cotton slipcovers, cushions, and pillows.

The lifestyle of beach living is unbeatable, with a quality that feels fuss-free and liberating—which means it's a style that translates easily to any location, waterside or not. The décor is fresh, inviting, and breezy.

To instill a home with these pleasures:

- think white—white furniture, white walls—to produce a clear background that has the feel of a stretch of white sand, setting the mood and the landscape;

- add narrow stripes for a subtle nautical feeling, and checks with the freshness of summer clothes;

- look for wood furniture in warm, honey tones;

- keep artwork minimal and lighthearted to maintain an open, upbeat look and mood;

- use carpets and baskets to bring in natural tones;

- turn to lightweight fabrics and slipcovers and light colors for a summery effect; in winter, add warmer throws in the same colors.

To the white base, add beach colors: Yellow and white pinstripes from the sun; blue and white for the sky; honey-color, whitewashed woods in sandy tones; sages that bring to mind sea grass.

smooth sailing

Fabrics have a special feeling that's fresh and smooth. Soft and natural cottons are the fabric of choice for upholstery, slipcovers, and pillows. Piping is the only detail—no flounces, ruffles or fringe—to send an understated message.

Beach living gains its warmth from the architectural backdrop of your interiors. Paint walls white to give the rooms clarity and a clean feeling. Floors can also be white for a seamless effect and for the additionally airy quality they instantly create. For a cottagey feeling, add beadboard to the walls, using it as wainscoting; keep it low—at or below windowsill level—to make the rest of the wall seem taller. Use glass interior doors whenever possible for an open effect; for privacy, fabric or lace panels can be attached. If you are fortunate enough to live on a beach, install an outdoor shower to make washing off sand a snap, and to have the everyday delight of looking up and seeing treetops and open sky.

sunshiny days

For a year-round summer feeling use an informal grouping such as these armchairs instead of traditional dining chairs, and a round table for its unceremonious, democratic quality. Choose a chandelier with simple styling and a fanciful feature—this one's coral tones and unadorned lights have a delightful aspect. Bring the beach inside with starfish and shells on ledges, and in baskets, vases, and frames. Instead of formal arrangements, display bundles of sea grass.

how to create
the look

Beach house style is about comfort and stress-free living. White starts the look, for walls and key furnishings—even honey-color woods have a white-wash. The emphasis of furnishings is practicality. Cotton upholstery, slipcovers, and pillows contain beach colors: sky blues, sunny yellows, and beach-grass greens. Relaxed upholstered pieces contribute to the mood, as do beach finds such as starfish and shells. Artwork is minimal for a breezy look.

beachcombing

A soothing lightness fills rooms with beach house style. Attain it with simple, unadorned pieces; with relaxed furniture such as wicker and rat-tan; and with easy accessories such as baskets and shells. Art, too, should have an airy quality, not just in subject matter, but in how it's framed and presented.

keys to successful style

1 Sofas should have a simple, easy-going shape to establish the mood of the rooms.   2 A round dining table has an informal quality, as does the pairing of a natural-tone top and white-painted pedestal base.
3 This wicker-look chair adds a summer porch feeling.   4 Natural baskets make simple, unpretentious catch-alls.   5 Artwork should reflect a lighthearted beach setting in presentation as well as content; here, a starfish "floating" in a shadowbox frame.   6 The first aim of furniture is function, as seen in this open coffee table with drawers.
7 Select white accessories to finish the theme, such as a simple lamp with an off-white shade.

1

2

3

4

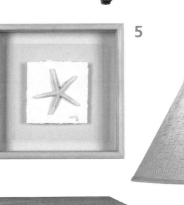

5

6

7

Beach colors—yellow, blue, white, and sage—bring ease to any home.

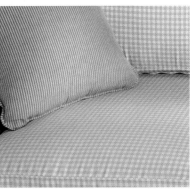

Like old-fashioned summer clothing, stripes and plaids add to the mood.

Because comfort is key, include cozy curl-ups, such as a Fair Isle throw.

Easy and practical — a rug with a tight weave and relaxed air.

kids' stuff

The opportunity to have fun and be free with style is what kids' rooms are all about, letting your imagination and that of your child soar. The best rooms are about combining two ideas—energy and attitude—to create the personality of an individualized space.

But a child's room also has to fulfill practical needs, such as storage, work, and play. And it needs to be flexible enough to grow with your child.

On the following pages you'll find everything you need to create the best rooms for boys and girls and babies.

room to grow

The energy: a balance of activity and rest. The attitude: creative and independent.

Boys and girls respond instantly to this bold and friendly look. Children love the bright colors, stripes, star-shape rugs, and the furniture on wheels. What you'll love is that the furniture is meant to grow with children through college: The bleached wood has an ageless appeal that takes easily to any bedcoverings, and the use of brushed metal hardware gives it an updated stylishness. Having some of the pieces on wheels means that they're easy to rearrange—a night table can wake up as a companion to the desk or rolled beside LEGOs™ or Barbie™ dolls for easy access to stored contents.

playing around

Choose a pattern with a cheerful quality that's ideal for any age. Here, it's cabana stripes, with practical, double-sided coverlets for an instant color change. Include whimsical accents—the felt pillow with appliquéd polka dots. A collection of creatures marches across a ledge as instant art and play inspiration.

sweet and pretty

The energy: imaginative and playful.
The attitude: gentle and inspiring.

The balancing act in a little girl's room is to make it sweet without going overboard into sugary. The way to achieve that is with classic furnishings that will look stylish through her teen years, and even when she's grown up, or when you want the room to double as a guest room. Here, the timeless approach is met with a panel bed that has a shell crown and pineapple finials. White paint makes the furniture enduring: avoid colors that become outdated quickly.

dressing up

Choose a theme for the room, and continue it in everything from bed linens to a lampshade. Here, the look is a romanticized idea of what a country girl would wear: a duvet with the appeal of a jean jacket, its opposite side a vintage rose print; pillows and sheets with a petticoat ruffle or crocheted hem; a quilted throw with rickrack trim. The red floral sham is a 1940s pattern. For an older child, switch the heart-themed pieces for more vintage florals.

babies and lullabies

The energy: soothing and tender.

The attitude: eye-catching and touching.

A baby's room can have terrific style without nursery-rhyme wallpaper or borders that will be too young by kindergarten. Think classics: a Shaker-style rocker; a changing table that converts to an open cottage-style dresser; a Victorian wicker bin that's a classic storage piece. The crib's clean design blends easily with the other furnishings. Continue a vintage Americana theme with wallpaper in a star pattern; prints of antique planes and cars; and old-fashioned toys. All in all, a room to stimulate a baby's interest in his or her surroundings, and complement a child's growing interests.

all-American baby

Vintage style is an ideal theme for a baby's room, with an old-fashioned sweetness and wonderful graphic appeal. The sheets and bumper have simple polka dots and rickrack, with a crib skirt that's a sophisticated matelassé. The red pillow is styled after a child's sweater and has hat pom-poms. A hooked rug adds atmosphere.

emphasis on accents

What sets a pleasant room apart from a stunning one is closing the distance between "almost-there" and "complete." It's the finishing touches that count once upholstery and fabric are in place. On these pages, our design consultants share their secrets, walking you through steps you'll want to take. You'll learn how to round out a room with style, warmth, and presence. We've focused on three key areas that require expertise: lighting; bedrooms; and decorative accessories for classic, contemporary, and country rooms. Here's your chance to see how design consultants bring life to a room and to learn how you can do it, too.

lighting 101

Not only does lighting allow us to function properly, but it also sets a mood—making it one of the most important aspects of style. Rooms require light that's evenly dispersed to prevent glare or dark corners. Since natural light is rarely sufficient, three levels of light are needed: overhead lighting for the most ambient lighting; floor lamps for the next fullest illumination; and table lamps or shorter floor lamps for task lighting, such as for reading. Three levels of light emerge: ceiling height, mid-height, and lower height, adding interest to a room. Uplights behind plants add additional interest and mood. Where possible, lights should be on a dimmer for control.

night and day

Seen here, the same room by night and by day. While daytime shows no need for artificial illumination to read and function easily in the space, night is a different story, with all three levels of light coming together to give the room the disbursement of light it needs to function and set an appealing mood.

211

the beauty
of a bedroom

A bedroom is one of the most rewarding rooms to style because of the number of textures, layers, and fabrics that are compiled. The story is almost always primarily about fabrics. Here, a step-by-step look at how a room with the beautiful framework of a rice-carved bed and bow canopy comes into its own.

A beautiful eighteenth century gown is the theme, and the bed is dressed with details that might accompany such a gown, in a rich yet understated palette of creams and taupes. The bed is layered with two duvets: a linen and cotton damask with outline quilting and an embroidered silk with covered buttons. Full groupings of decorative pillows further enhance the look. The bed is then draped with custom-made cut-velvet sheer panels, with gentle ties to the canopy and fringed tassel tie-backs. The panels are puddled gracefully on the floor, like the train of a dress.

Next, the rest of the room is adorned: an eighteenth century-style portrait; an armchair given a frock-like, gently striped and fitted slipcover—with ties that give the impression of ribbons; an ornately patterned and colored Shah Abbas design rug; curtains in a simple yet formal design with a boxed valance; a side table topped with a clutch of white roses; and a white Regency-inspired lamp with valance detailing.

deluxe dressmaker details

Finishing details make the effect even richer. There is the pleasure of contrasting textures, such as the linen and cotton damask pillows with the impressive shirred corners of a ruffle on one, and precise box pleats on another. Covered buttons and woven cording provide beautiful textures, while a velvet tassel has the presence of a sash, an idea further borne out by the gentle train of the canopy panels.

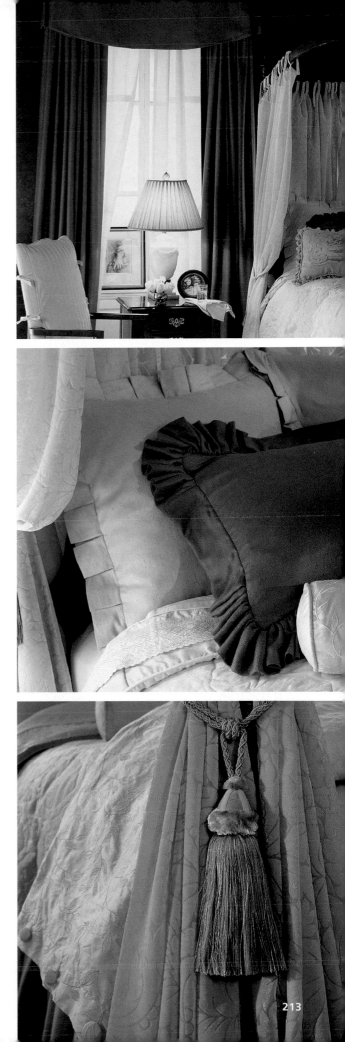

the ABCs of accents

Starting here, nine pages show how traditional, contemporary, and country styles are given distinct styling. On these two pages, the starting point is a table or bureau. Then, accessories are brought in.

In each case, the styling points are:

- balance—no one item should be overpowering;

- finishes—having a selection of tones creates interest;

- varying heights—to give the tableaux energy;

- consideration for the surrounding elements, whether they're paintings, drapes, or a background of white upholstery.

beautiful presentations

For the classic look on the opposite page, accessories are chosen with simple shapes that don't compete with the ornate carving of the console, but that match the strength of the piece. For the island look, the lightness of glass over a rattan-top coffee table continues in the simplicity of a rich-tone wood tray with bold color accents, and a woven suitcase with an intriguing vintage quality. In the eighteenth-century look, the formality of an inlaid dresser is accentuated by a gilt-frame mirror, and classical pieces such as the urn-shape lamp and Federal-style clock.

Contemporary rooms require careful consideration because in these more pared-down environments, every element stands out. Each of these three looks was built around one piece. On the opposite page, artwork is the inspiration. From there, a sofa is selected in simple yet graceful lines. Paint is chosen to enhance the soft gold of the art, with accessories bringing out additional colors. On this page, top, the starting point is the dark-tone book shelf with its unusual open back. The scale of the art balances the bookshelf and brings out the red tones of the wood. Further balance comes from the slim metal lamp. This page, below, the bold geometrics of the mirror frame is a wonderful match with the Art Deco influences of the chest of drawers and accessories.

color concepts

Color has dramatic presence in contemporary rooms. Wall colors—gold, gray, and deep blue—are in perfect harmony with the mood of the key element of each room, providing a more vivid presence. Artwork might influence color in a room, but it does not dictate it to the point where the room looks overmatched to the art—a mere hint of influence is chic.

217

Country styling has a warmth and friendliness that feels natural but is, in fact, carefully built in. Opposite, the pairing of blue and white is almost always key to Swedish country. Here, even though the dresser is large, its Swedish lineage requires sweeter detailing, as seen in the bell lamp and delicate blue and white accents, lower in scale to offset the dresser's height. For the all-American country look, a red sofa insists on robust art and bold accessories such as the amplified ticking pattern and large coffee table. The Arts and Crafts-style sideboard requires more careful composition: the four botanical prints are hung low to fully complement the piece. The vase and lamp bring slim vertical lines while the low bowl and glass cloche make a balanced foursome.

attention for walls

Notice how wall décor adds balance not only to the primary piece of furniture but also to the whole room. In the Swedish look, an oval mirror balances the space between the dresser and the ceiling. In the American country room, flag artwork provides horizontal stretch. For the Arts and Crafts room, four botanicals enhance the beauty of the sideboard: hung four across they underscore the width, and hung low, they play up its height.

219

ETHAN ALLEN
directory

UNITED STATES

Alabama

Birmingham
Ethan Allen Home Interiors
1069 Montgomery Highway

Dothan
Ethan Allen Home Interiors
3282 Montgomery Highway

Huntsville
Ethan Allen Home Interiors
3017 South Memorial Parkway

Mobile
Ethan Allen Home Interiors
4023 Airport Boulevard

Montgomery
Ethan Allen Home Interiors
3300 Eastern Boulevard

Arizona

Glendale
Ethan Allen Home Interiors
7760 West Bell Road

Mesa
Ethan Allen Home Interiors
1710 South Alma School Road

Phoenix
Ethan Allen Home Interiors
5301 North 16th Street

Scottsdale
Ethan Allen Home Interiors
11201 North Scottsdale Road

Tucson
Ethan Allen Home Interiors
5621 North Oracle Road

Arkansas

Little Rock
Ethan Allen Home Interiors
12301 Chenal Parkway

California

Artesia
Ethan Allen Home Interiors
11720 East South Street

Concord
Ethan Allen Home Interiors
2080 Diamond Boulevard

Costa Mesa
Ethan Allen Home Interiors
1835 Newport Boulevard
Suite C 139

220

Fairfield
Ethan Allen Home Interiors
5111 Business Center Drive

Fresno
Ethan Allen Home Interiors
3011 East Shields Avenue

Glendale
Ethan Allen Home Interiors
300 North Brand Boulevard

Laguna Niguel
Ethan Allen Home Interiors
28031 Greenfield Drive

La Mesa
Ethan Allen Home Interiors
8185 Fletcher Parkway

Mill Valley
Ethan Allen Home Interiors
1060 Redwood Highway

Modesto
Ethan Allen Home Interiors
3900 Sisk Road

Montclair
Ethan Allen Home Interiors
5001 South Plaza Lane

Mountain View
Ethan Allen Home Interiors
861 East El Camino Real

Newark
Ethan Allen Home Interiors
5763 Stevenson Boulevard

Northridge
Ethan Allen Home Interiors
8750 Tampa Avenue

Pasadena
Ethan Allen Home Interiors
445 North Rosemead Boulevard

Pleasanton
Ethan Allen Home Interiors
4230 Rosewood Drive

Puente Hills
Ethan Allen Home Interiors
4230 Rosewood Drive
City of Industry

Redding
Ethan Allen Home Interiors
307 Park Marina Circle

Sacramento
Ethan Allen Home Interiors
525 Fulton Avenue

Ethan Allen Home Interiors
5130 Madison Avenue

Salinas
Ethan Allen Home Interiors
1425 North Davis Road

San Bernardino
Ethan Allen Home Interiors
1363 South E Street

San Diego
Ethan Allen Home Interiors
7341 Clairemont Mesa Boulevard

San Jose
Ethan Allen Home Interiors
2500 Fontaine Road

San Marcos
Ethan Allen Home Interiors
1040 Los Vallecitos Boulevard

San Mateo
Ethan Allen Home Interiors
3020 Bridgepointe Parkway

Santa Ana
Ethan Allen Home Interiors
2101 North Tustin Avenue

Santa Rosa
Ethan Allen Home Interiors
2503 Cleveland Avenue

Saratoga
Ethan Allen Home Interiors
5285 Prospect Road

Thousand Oaks
Ethan Allen Home Interiors
111 South Westlake Boulevard
Suite 103

Torrance
Ethan Allen Home Interiors
2700 West Sepulveda Boulevard

Valencia
Ethan Allen Home Interiors
26350 Citrus Street

Ventura
Ethan Allen Home Interiors
3970 East Main Street

West Los Angeles
Ethan Allen Home Interiors
11419 Santa Monica Boulevard

Colorado

Aurora
Ethan Allen Home Interiors
1690 South Chambers Road

Colorado Springs
Ethan Allen Home Interiors
7298 North Academy Boulevard

Fort Collins
Ethan Allen Home Interiors
4636 South Mason Street

Littleton
Ethan Allen Home Interiors
4151 East County Line Road

Westminster
Ethan Allen Home Interiors
8780 West 101st Avenue and
Wadsworth Parkway

Connecticut

Canton
Ethan Allen Home Interiors
135 Albany Turnpike

Clinton
Ethan Allen Home Interiors
2 Killingworth Turnpike

Danbury
Ethan Allen Home Interiors
Ethan Allen Drive

Groton
Ethan Allen Home Interiors
721 Long Hill Road

Manchester
Ethan Allen Home Interiors
49 Hale Road

Milford
Ethan Allen Home Interiors
1620 Boston Post Road

Norwalk
Ethan Allen Home Interiors
556 Main Avenue, Route 7

Southington
Ethan Allen Home Interiors
228 Queen Street

Stamford
Ethan Allen Home Interiors
2046 West Main Street

Delaware

Wilmington
Ethan Allen Home Interiors
4507 Kirkwood Highway

Florida

Altamonte Springs
Ethan Allen Home Interiors
249 West Highway 436
Suite 1033

Boca Raton
Ethan Allen Home Interiors
9200 West Glades Road
Boca Lyons Plaza

Fort Lauderdale
Ethan Allen Home Interiors
2900 North Federal Highway

Fort Myers
Ethan Allen Home Interiors
16240 South Tamiami Trail

Jacksonville West
Ethan Allen Home Interiors
7666 Blanding Boulevard

Jacksonville East
Ethan Allen Home Interiors
10452 Phillips Highway

Lakeland
Ethan Allen Home Interiors
4505 South Florida Avenue

Melbourne
Ethan Allen Home Interiors
2705 North Harbor City Boulevard

Miami
Ethan Allen Home Interiors
15053 South Dixie Highway

Naples
Ethan Allen Home Interiors
3000 North Tamiami Trail

Orlando
Ethan Allen Home Interiors
9677 South Orange Blossom Trail

Ormond Beach
Ethan Allen Home Interiors
450 South Yonge Street
U.S. Highway 1

Osprey
Ethan Allen Home Interiors
1200 South Tamiami Trail

Pembroke Pines
Ethan Allen Home Interiors
13680 Pines Boulevard

Pensacola
Ethan Allen Home Interiors
6235 North Davis Highway #101B

Pinellas Park
Ethan Allen Home Interiors
8901 U.S. Highway 19 North

Port Richey
Ethan Allen Home Interiors
9825 U.S. Highway 19

Stuart
Ethan Allen Home Interiors
1000 NW Federal Highway

Tampa
Ethan Allen Home Interiors
6200 North Dale Mabry Highway

Ethan Allen Home Interiors
10015 Adamo Drive

Ethan Allen Home Interiors
8314 Citrus Park Parkway

Vero Beach
Ethan Allen Home Interiors
8505 20th Street
Route 60

West Palm Beach
Ethan Allen Home Interiors
2231 Palm Beach Lakes Boulevard

Georgia

Alpharetta
Ethan Allen Home Interiors
6751 North Point Parkway

Atlanta
Ethan Allen Home Interiors
3221 Peachtree Road, NE

Augusta
Ethan Allen Home Interiors
3437 Wrightsboro Road

Buford
Ethan Allen Home Interiors
1885 Mall of Georgia Boulevard

Kennesaw
Ethan Allen Home Interiors
1005 Barrett Parkway

Peachtree City
Ethan Allen Home Interiors
101 Market Place Boulevard

Smyrna
Ethan Allen Home Interiors
2205 Cobb Parkway

Idaho

Boise
Ethan Allen Home Interiors
400 North Cole Road

Illinois

Arlington Heights
Ethan Allen Home Interiors
1211 East Rand Road

Batavia
Ethan Allen Home Interiors
16 North Batavia Avenue

Bloomington
Ethan Allen Home Interiors
1344 East Empire

Chicago
Ethan Allen Home Interiors
1700 North Halsted

Countryside
Ethan Allen Home Interiors
6001 South LaGrange Road

Fairview Heights
Ethan Allen Home Interiors
455 Salem Place

Gurnee
Ethan Allen Home Interiors
3550 West Grand Avenue
at Route 41

Orland Park
Ethan Allen Home Interiors
15500 Harlem Avenue

Peoria
Ethan Allen Home Interiors
613 West Lake Street

Rockford
Ethan Allen Home Interiors
4720 East State Street

Skokie
Ethan Allen Home Interiors
10001 Skokie Boulevard

Wheaton
Ethan Allen Home Interiors
820 East Roosevelt Road

Indiana

Evansville
Ethan Allen Home Interiors
7500 Eagle Crest Boulevard

Fort Wayne
Ethan Allen Home Interiors
1121 West Washington Center Road

Indianapolis
Ethan Allen Home Interiors
4905 East 82nd Street

Merrillville
Ethan Allen Home Interiors
8000 Broadway

Mishawaka
Ethan Allen Home Interiors
5225 North Main Street

Iowa

Cedar Rapids
Ethan Allen Home Interiors
1170 Twixt Town Road

Davenport
Ethan Allen Home Interiors
301 West Kimberly Road

Des Moines
Ethan Allen Home Interiors
7700 Hickman Road

Kansas

Overland Park
Ethan Allen Home Interiors
7090 West 135th Street

Wichita
Ethan Allen Home Interiors
416 North Rock Road

Kentucky

Lexington
Ethan Allen Home Interiors
2191 Nicholasville Road

Louisville
Ethan Allen Home Interiors
9801 Linn Station Road

Paducah
Ethan Allen Home Interiors
114 North Third Street

Louisiana

Baton Rouge
Ethan Allen Home Interiors
8560 Florida Boulevard

Metairie
Ethan Allen Home Interiors
5300 Veterans Boulevard

Shreveport
Ethan Allen Home Interiors
8824 Youree Drive

Maine

South Portland
Ethan Allen Home Interiors
160 Western Avenue

Maryland

Annapolis
Ethan Allen Home Interiors
2401 Solomons Island Road

Baltimore
Ethan Allen Home Interiors
6612 Baltimore National Pike

Frederick
Ethan Allen Home Interiors
5500 Buckeystown Pike

Rockville
Ethan Allen Home Interiors
1800 East Rockville Pike

Towson
Ethan Allen Home Interiors
8727 Loch Raven Boulevard

Massachusetts

Auburn
Ethan Allen Home Interiors
619 Southbridge Street
Route 12

Burlington
Ethan Allen Home Interiors
34 Cambridge Street

Hyannis
Ethan Allen Home Interiors
1520 Route 132

Natick
Ethan Allen Home Interiors
625 Worcester Road
Route 9

North Andover
Ethan Allen Home Interiors
419 Andover Street

Quincy
Ethan Allen Home Interiors
840 Willard Street

Saugus
Ethan Allen Home Interiors
636 Broadway, Route 1

Swansea
Ethan Allen Home Interiors
2241 GAR Highway

Michigan

Ann Arbor
Ethan Allen Home Interiors
820 West Eisenhower
Cranbrook Village Parkway

Auburn Hills
Ethan Allen Home Interiors
100 Brown Road

Birmingham
Ethan Allen Home Interiors
275 North Old Woodward Avenue

Grand Rapids
Ethan Allen Home Interiors
3450 28th Street SE

Kalamazoo
Ethan Allen Home Interiors
6025 West Main Street

Lansing
Ethan Allen Home Interiors
8439 West Saginaw Road

Livonia
Ethan Allen Home Interiors
15700 Middlebelt Road

Novi
Ethan Allen Home Interiors
42845 Twelve Mile Road

Saginaw
Ethan Allen Home Interiors
5570 Bay Road

Sterling Heights
Ethan Allen Home Interiors
13725 Lakeside Circle

Traverse City
Ethan Allen Home Interiors
862 South Garfield Avenue

Minnesota

Eagan
Ethan Allen Home Interiors
1270 Promenade Place

Edina
Ethan Allen Home Interiors
7101 France Avenue South

Minnetonka
Ethan Allen Home Interiors
12320 Wayzata Boulevard

St. Paul
Ethan Allen Home Interiors
1111 East Highway 36

Missouri

Chesterfield
Ethan Allen Home Interiors
15464 Olive Boulevard

Columbia
Ethan Allen Home Interiors
400 North Stadium Boulevard

Independence
Ethan Allen Home Interiors
18680 East 39th Street South

Kirkwood
Ethan Allen Home Interiors
10465 Manchester Road

Liberty
Ethan Allen Home Interiors
1 North Water Street

Springfield
Ethan Allen Home Interiors
2825 South Glenstone
Battlefield Mall

Montana

Billings
Ethan Allen Home Interiors
3220 First Avenue North

Nebraska

Lincoln
Ethan Allen Home Interiors
70th and Van Dorn

Omaha
Ethan Allen Home Interiors
10720 Pacific Street

Nevada

Henderson
Ethan Allen Home Interiors
249 North Stephanie Street

Las Vegas
Ethan Allen Home Interiors
1540 South Rainbow Boulevard

Reno
Ethan Allen Home Interiors
3445 Kietzke Lane

New Hampshire

Bedford
Ethan Allen Home Interiors
192 Route 101 West

Plaistow
Ethan Allen Home Interiors
Route 125

Portsmouth
Ethan Allen Home Interiors
755 Lafayette Road
Route 1

New Jersey

Brick
Ethan Allen Home Interiors
110 Brick Plaza

Deptford
Ethan Allen Home Interiors
1692-F Clements Bridge Road
Locust Grove Plaza

East Brunswick
Ethan Allen Home Interiors
260 Route 18 North

Eatontown
Ethan Allen Home Interiors
164 Route 35 at South Street

Lawrenceville
Ethan Allen Home Interiors
2470 Brunswick Pike

Maple Shade
Ethan Allen Home Interiors
489 Route 38 West

Mays Landing
Ethan Allen Home Interiors
400 Consumer Square
2300 Wrangleboro Road

Princeton
Ethan Allen Home Interiors
3542 US Route 1 North

River Edge
Ethan Allen Home Interiors
Route 4 East and Main Street

Secaucus
Ethan Allen Home Interiors
850 Patterson Plank Road

Somerville
Ethan Allen Home Interiors
870 Route 22 East

Watchung
Ethan Allen Home Interiors
1541 Route 22

Wayne
Ethan Allen Home Interiors
475 Route 46 West

Whippany
Ethan Allen Home Interiors
245 Route 10

New Mexico

Albuquerque
Ethan Allen Home Interiors
12521 Montgomery Boulevard NE

New York

Amherst
Ethan Allen Home Interiors
3875 Sheridan Drive

Bay Shore
Ethan Allen Home Interiors
456 Montauk Highway

Clifton Park
Ethan Allen Home Interiors
15 Park Avenue, Shopper's World

DeWitt
Ethan Allen Home Interiors
Dewey Avenue and East Genesee

Forest Hills
Ethan Allen Home Interiors
112-33 Queens Boulevard

Garden City
Ethan Allen Home Interiors
750 Stewart Avenue

Hartsdale
Ethan Allen Home Interiors
152 South Central Avenue

Huntington Station
Ethan Allen Home Interiors
30 West Jericho Turnpike

Lake Grove
Ethan Allen Home Interiors
2758 Middle Country Road
Suite 2

Lynbrook
Ethan Allen Home Interiors
881 Sunrise Highway

Manhasset
Ethan Allen Home Interiors
1575 Northern Boulevard

Nanuet
Ethan Allen Home Interiors
300 East Route 59 and
Smith Street

Newburgh
Ethan Allen Home Interiors
94 North Plank Road

New York
Ethan Allen Home Interiors
1107 Third Avenue and
65th Street

Ethan Allen Home Interiors
192 Lexington Avenue and
32nd Street

Ethan Allen Home Interiors
103 West End Avenue

Schenectady
Ethan Allen Home Interiors
2191 Central Avenue

Staten Island
Ethan Allen Home Interiors
2275 Richmond Avenue
Unit 21-23

Vestal
Ethan Allen Home Interiors
124 Sycamore Road

Victor
Ethan Allen Home Interiors
32 Eastview Mall Drive

North Carolina

Asheville
Ethan Allen Home Interiors
Interstate 26 at Brevard Road

Cary
Ethan Allen Home Interiors
5717 Dillard Drive

Charlotte
Ethan Allen Home Interiors
7025 Smith Corner Boulevard

Pineville
Ethan Allen Home Interiors
11516 Carolina Place Parkway

Raleigh
Ethan Allen Home Interiors
7010 Glenwood Avenue

Wilmington
Ethan Allen Home Interiors
818 South College Road

North Dakota

Fargo
Ethan Allen Home Interiors
1429 42nd Street SW

Ohio

Akron
Ethan Allen Home Interiors
55 Springside Drive

Centerville
Ethan Allen Home Interiors
821 Miamisburg at Centerville Road

Cincinnati
Ethan Allen Home Interiors
12151 Royal Point Drive

Kettering
Ethan Allen Home Interiors
1000 East Dorothy Lane

Mentor
Ethan Allen Home Interiors
7850 Mentor Avenue

North Olmsted
Ethan Allen Home Interiors
26127 Lorain Road

Reynoldsburg
Ethan Allen Home Interiors
6411 East Main Street

Springdale
Ethan Allen Home Interiors
11285 Princeton Pike

Toledo
Ethan Allen Home Interiors
6755 West Central Avenue

Woodmere
Ethan Allen Home Interiors
27079 Chagrin Boulevard

Worthington
Ethan Allen Home Interiors
6767 North High Street

Youngstown
Ethan Allen Home Interiors
8040 Market Street

Oklahoma

Oklahoma City
Ethan Allen Home Interiors
222 South Portland

Tulsa
Ethan Allen Home Interiors
6006 South Sheridan

Oregon

Beaverton
Ethan Allen Home Interiors
2800 NW Town Center Drive
Tanasbourne Town Center

Lake Oswego
Ethan Allen Home Interiors
15383 SW Bangy Road

Springfield
Ethan Allen Home Interiors
3150 Gateway Loop

Pennsylvania

Allentown
Ethan Allen Home Interiors
5064 Hamilton Boulevard

Altoona
Ethan Allen Home Interiors
1 Sheraton Drive

Concordville
Ethan Allen Home Interiors
Routes 1 and 322

Dickson City
Ethan Allen Home Interiors
930 Viewmont Drive

East Petersburg
Ethan Allen Home Interiors
5139 Manheim Pike

Erie
Ethan Allen Home Interiors
7520 Peach Street

Langhorne
Ethan Allen Home Interiors
510 Oxford Valley Road

McMurray
Ethan Allen Home Interiors
2917 Washington Road

Monroeville
Ethan Allen Home Interiors
4685 William Penn Highway

Montgomeryville
Ethan Allen Home Interiors
668 Bethlehem Pike
Route 309

Paoli
Ethan Allen Home Interiors
1616 Lancaster Avenue

Wexford
Ethan Allen Home Interiors
14010 Perry Highway

Willow Grove
Ethan Allen Home Interiors
2522 Moreland Road

Rhode Island

Warwick
Ethan Allen Home Interiors
1775 Bald Hill Road

South Carolina

Charleston
Ethan Allen Home Interiors
1821A Sam Rittenberg Boulevard

Columbia
Ethan Allen Home Interiors
101 Harbison Boulevard

Greenville
Ethan Allen Home Interiors
7 Park Woodruff Drive

South Dakota

Sioux Falls
Ethan Allen Home Interiors
2300 West 49th Street

Tennessee

Brentwood
Ethan Allen Home Interiors
1805 Mallory Lane

Chatanooga
Ethan Allen Home Interiors
7351 Commons Boulevard

Cordova
Ethan Allen Home Interiors
1820 North Germantown Parkway

Knoxville
Ethan Allen Home Interiors
10001 Kingston Pike

Nashville
Ethan Allen Home Interiors
2031 Richard Jones Road

Texas

Austin
Ethan Allen Home Interiors
2913 Anderson Lane

Beaumont
Ethan Allen Home Interiors
4755 East Texas Freeway

Corpus Christi
Ethan Allen Home Interiors
4325 South Padre Island Drive

Dallas
Ethan Allen Home Interiors
13920 North Dallas Parkway

Denton
Ethan Allen Home Interiors
200 West Oak Street

El Paso
Ethan Allen Home Interiors
5664 North Mesa Street

Friendswood
Ethan Allen Home Interiors
19240 Gulf Freeway

Frisco
Ethan Allen Home Interiors
2100 Parkwood Boulevard

Houston
Ethan Allen Home Interiors
4081R Westheimer Road

Ethan Allen Home Interiors
11431 Katy Freeway

Ethan Allen Home Interiors
16525 North Freeway

Ethan Allen Home Interiors
17685 Tomball Parkway

Hurst
Ethan Allen Home Interiors
633 NE Loop 820

Lewisville
Ethan Allen Home Interiors
2521 Stemmons Freeway

Mesquite
Ethan Allen Home Interiors
2330 Interstate 30

Richardson
Ethan Allen Home Interiors
305 South Central Expressway

San Antonio
Ethan Allen Home Interiors
2819 NW Loop 410

Stafford
Ethan Allen Home Interiors
12625 Southwest Freeway

Tyler
Ethan Allen Home Interiors
815 West Southwest Loop 323

Utah

Salt Lake City
Ethan Allen Home Interiors
4545 South 900 East

Vermont

Shelburne
Ethan Allen Home Interiors
2735 Shelburne Road

Virginia

Fredericksburg
Ethan Allen Home Interiors
1480 Carl D. Silver Parkway

Glen Allen
Ethan Allen Home Interiors
10300 West Broad Street

Potomac Falls
Ethan Allen Home Interiors
45460 Dulles Crossing Plaza

Roanoke
Ethan Allen Home Interiors
4118 Electric Road
Route 419 S.W.

Springfield
Ethan Allen Home Interiors
6774 Springfield Mall

Vienna (Tyson's Corner)
Ethan Allen Home Interiors
8520-A Leesburg Pike

Virginia Beach
Ethan Allen Home Interiors
1554 Laskin Road, Unit 110
Hilltop East Shopping Center

Williamsburg
Ethan Allen Home Interiors
3032-1 Richmond Road

Washington

Lynnwood
Ethan Allen Home Interiors
4029 Alderwood Mall Boulevard

Redmond
Ethan Allen Home Interiors
2209 NE Bellevue-Redmond Road

Spokane
Ethan Allen Home Interiors
5511 East Third Avenue

Tukwila
Ethan Allen Home Interiors
17333 Southcenter Parkway

Wisconsin

Appleton
Ethan Allen Home Interiors
144 Mall Drive

Brookfield
Ethan Allen Home Interiors
14750 West Capitol Drive

Green Bay
Ethan Allen Home Interiors
2350 South Oneida Street

Greenfield
Ethan Allen Home Interiors
7740 West Layton Avenue

Madison
Ethan Allen Home Interiors
5302 Verona Road

Mequon
Ethan Allen Home Interiors
10900 North Port Washington Road

Wausau
Ethan Allen Home Interiors
2107 Robin Lane

INTERNATIONAL

Bangladesh

Dhaka
Ethan Allen Home Interiors
House 3, Road 94, Gulshan 2

Brazil

São Paulo
Ethan Allen Home Interiors
Alameda Gabriel Monteiro Da Silva, 949

Canada

Burlington, Ontario
Ethan Allen Home Interiors
3225 Fairview Street

Calgary, Alberta
Ethan Allen Home Interiors
32 Mayfair Place
6707 Elbow Drive SW

Coquitlam, B.C.
Ethan Allen Home Interiors
1555 United Boulevard

Edmonton, Alberta
Ethan Allen Home Interiors
17010 90th Avenue

Mississauga, Ontario
Ethan Allen Home Interiors
2161 Dundas Street West

Pickering, Ontario
Ethan Allen Home Interiors
1755 Pickering Parkway

Richmond, B.C.
Ethan Allen Home Interiors
2633 Sweden Way

Thornhill, Ontario
Ethan Allen Home Interiors
8134 Yonge Street

Toronto, Ontario
Ethan Allen Home Interiors
1819 Yonge Street

Dominican Republic

Piantini, Santo Domingo
Ethan Allen Home Interiors
Gustavo Mejia Ricart #124-A

Egypt

Heliopolis, Cairo
Ethan Allen Home Interiors
2 Abdel Aziz El Hawary Street

Mohandiseen, Cairo
Ethan Allen Home Interiors
14 Wadi El Nil Street

Japan

Chiba
Ethan Allen Home Interiors
IDC 1-2-1 Tsudanuma
Narashino Shi

Osaka
Ethan Allen Home Interiors
1-17-28 Minami Horie, Nishi-Ku

Ethan Allen Home Interiors
IDC ATC Building 8F
2-1-10 Nanko-Kita, Suminoe-Ku

Kasukabe, Saitama
Ethan Allen Home Interiors
1-9-7 Tyuou

Tokyo
Ethan Allen Home Interiors
IDC TFT Building 4F
3-1 Ariake, Koto-Ku

Kuwait

Kuwait City
Ethan Allen Home Interiors
Al Rai, Hassawi Street

Mexico

Mexico City
Ethan Allen Home Interiors
Insurgentes Sur 1618

Philippines

Mandaluyong City, Manila
Ethan Allen Home Interiors
Pioneer Street at Reliance Street

South Korea

Kangnam-Ku, Seoul
Ethan Allen Home Interiors
91-12 Chungdam-dong

Chung-Ku, Taegu
Ethan Allen Home Interiors
25-21 Daebong 1 Dong

Taiwan

Kao-hsiung
Ethan Allen Home Interiors
No. 176 Ho-Tun Road 4F
Chen-Chin

Shing Chung, Taipei
Ethan Allen Home Interiors
186 Section 1
Chung Shang Road

United Arab Emirates

Dubai
Ethan Allen Home Interiors
Century Mall
Jumeirah Beach Road

United Kingdom

Bromley, Kent
Ethan Allen Home Interiors
Hanover Place
44 High Street

Kingston Upon Thames, Surrey
Ethan Allen Home Interiors
31 Thames Street